A Really Basic Introduction to

Accountancy

By Michael Lambarth

Other books available in this series include:

A Really Basic Introduction to English Law and the English Legal System

A Really Basic Introduction to English Contract Law

A Really Basic Introduction to Company Law

A Really Basic Introduction to Value Added Tax

A Really Basic Introduction to Income Tax

A Really Basic Introduction to Capital Gains Tax

Contents

Chapter 1 – Introduction

Welcome to 'A Really Basic Introduction to Accountancy'. Have you ever tried to find introductory books about complicated topics, only to be completely lost after a few pages? Usually, the author starts the book by explaining how basic the book will be, and then appears to forget this altogether on the very next page when he or she starts to use words which you do not understand. Having stated that no previous knowledge is required, they very quickly start to assume that you know the meaning of specific terms, or they say that it would be helpful to know a bit about some other subject before reading the book. The fact that you have purchased a book which was described as a basic introduction to the subject seems to evade them completely.

This book is exactly what it says it is; a really basic introduction to accountancy. No previous knowledge of accounting is needed. I will explain all terms in full as we go along and will not try to impress you with my knowledge of complex terminology. This book will give you a good understanding of accounts at a basic level. It will help you understand your own business's accounts and finances. It will also help you if you are undertaking any course of study where knowledge of accounts is required, such as accounting, business, management, law or finance. Needless to say, an introductory book of this nature does have its limitations. After reading through it, you will not be able to give detailed accounting advice to other people. Nor will you understand the subject in depth, or be able to talk to a professional adviser on their own terms. It is, after all, a really basic introduction to the topic.

So who am I to think that I can write such a book? Well, I am a qualified solicitor and used to work for one of the big UK accountancy firms. I also have respected tax qualifications, and I am a qualified higher education teacher. Hopefully I therefore have the skills needed to convey this subject in a clear and concise manner. I have spent many hours explaining the principles in this book to students, colleagues and clients, so I am convinced you will be able to follow what I am saying.

I have tried to keep this book as short as possible, so that it is manageable, and so that you don't lose interest or feel intimidated after just a couple of chapters. The other thing I have done is to try to keep things real and practical. Accountancy is a difficult enough subject to grasp, without trying to do so in the abstract. Each chapter builds upon the last, introducing and then expanding on different ideas as the book progresses. This means that your understanding is automatically consolidated as you read and that you should be able to read this book from start to finish and end up with a pretty good understanding of what is going on. I hope that you will end up with a confident, basic understanding of the subject.

Please remember that this book is a really basic introduction to business accounts. It should give you a good understanding of the basics and help you to understand your own affairs. It should also give you a good foundation for further study if that is your aim. You should not use it as a substitute for advice from a qualified expert.

I hope you enjoy the book.

Chapter 2 – Where to Start?

Where to start? That is always a difficult question to answer with any subject, but especially with a subject as wide as accountancy. What I have decided to do here is to run through much of the basic accountancy process in its entirety in one chapter. Wait, don't give up… I think you might just find this a very helpful way to approach things. I'll take you through it step by step and explain everything as I go. Then, the rest of the book will go back over each concept in more detail, by which stage you will have an idea of how it all fits together and why things are happening.

Still with me? Good. Then let's get on with it.

Let me introduce you to Abigail. She is 22 years old and has just completed a photography degree at university. She now intends to set up her own business as a photographer. She plans to start her business with some savings which she has managed to put together.

One of the first things Abigail will need to think about in accounting terms is when her business will actually start trading. Let's say she decides to start trading on 1st June XXX1. From that date she can work out when her first year of trading will finish – on the 31st May XXX2. This date will be her year-end. Most businesses tend to work in years as it is a convenient measure of time in which to assess financial performance, and also it helps the accounts to stay 'in line' with the tax year regime. We won't be looking at taxation in too much detail in this book, but it will be referred to here and there. One initial point to note is that Abigail will no doubt hope to make a profit from her business, and that profit will potentially be subject to income tax. In effect, her profit replaces the salary that she might have earned had she chosen to work for someone else. In the same way that her salary would have been subject to income tax, so will the profit she makes from her own business.

Going back to her year-end, which we have said will be 31st May XXX2, we would refer to the period 1st June XXX1 to 31st May XXX2 as Abigail's first accounting period. It ends on 31st May XXX2, which is her year-end, or accounting reference date (often abbreviated to ARD). Note that Abigail could choose a different year-end (or accounting reference date), so that her first accounting period would be shorter than one year, but for simplicity let's leave it at one year exactly.

So Abigail decides to start her business on 1st June XXX1. In the months leading up to that date she will no doubt have carried out some market research, planned what she needs to buy, thought about advertising, decided how much she will charge for her services and so on. There is much to think about and plan when setting up a new business, even a relatively simple one. Many of these decisions will help her to decide how much money she needs to start her business with. Let's assume that for now Abigail has decided that she will need to buy a good quality camera, a laptop, a printer and some ink. For now she will operate her business from home and will not incur any expenses in that respect.

Today is 1st June and Abigail's first day in business as a self-employed photographer. She arrives at the bank at 9 o'clock in the morning and opens a business bank account. She calls her business simply, 'Abigail Photography' and this is the name in which the bank opens her account. She has chosen this bank because it offers her free banking for her first year (banks often charge for the operation of a business account). Abigail withdraws £3,000 from her personal savings account and pays it into the new bank account for her business. This gives rise to her first accounting entry.

Accountancy is based on a system called 'double entry bookkeeping'. As the name suggests, each transaction that a business is involved with gives rise to two entries. These entries will be made in two different accounts, or 'ledgers'. Perhaps the most important ledger is the cash ledger, in which movements of money are recorded. Although it is called the cash ledger, it is not just movements of cash that are recorded in there, but also movements on the business's bank account (debit card transactions, direct debits, cheques and so on).

A ledger is usually represented like this:

Cash

Date	Details	Dr	Cr	Balance

This is the cash ledger. There are several columns to each ledger. The first column records the date of each transaction and the second column records the details – usually the name of the account in which the other side of the transaction is recorded (remember, we said each transaction gives rise to two entries). Next, there are two columns which record debits (dr) (deductions from the ledger) and credits (cr) (additions to the ledger). The final column records the running balance on the account.

Going back to Abigail, we said that the payment of her own money into the business bank account gave rise to an accounting entry. In fact it gives rise to two entries of course, because double entry bookkeeping always requires two entries. One will be a credit and one will be a debit, and the two entries will be equal and opposite. In that way the accounts remain balanced. Let's have a look at what I mean.

Here is Abigail's cash ledger after she has paid in the £3,000 to her business bank account.

Cash

Date	Details	Dr	Cr	Balance
01/06	Capital	3000		3000dr

This immediately raises some questions. First of all, why does the ledger have a debit balance? This seems to suggest that Abigail's business is overdrawn at the bank when we know that is not the case! She is in fact £3,000 in credit. Also, what on earth is capital?

Before we answer those questions, let's check out the other side of the entry. This goes to the capital ledger and looks like this.

Capital

Date	Details	Dr	Cr	Balance
01/06	Cash		3000	3000cr

So we can see clearly that the entries in the cash and capital ledgers are opposite (one is a debit, on the left hand side and one is a credit, on the right hand side) and that they are equal in size (both

£3,000). The basic rules have therefore been followed; the accounts will 'balance' because they show a £3,000 credit and a £3,000 debit. Both sides are equal and opposite, and therefore balance. You could imagine them as weights on opposite sides of a set of scales.

Going back to our two questions, let's deal with the easier of the two first. What is capital? Capital is simply a name for the amount of money (and potentially other things) that a person invests into their business. In Abigail's case she has invested £3,000 into her business, all in cash. Soon she will buy a camera for the business. In reality of course, she would probably already have a camera. If, rather than investing £3,000 in cash into her business, she invested £2,200 in cash plus a camera worth £800, then the figure in the two ledgers above would be £2,200. We would then need to make similar entries for the camera at £800. These latter entries would be a credit in the capital ledger, taking the balance on that ledger to £3,000, and a debit in the 'Cameras' ledger, to show that the business owned a camera worth £800. We'll come back to this later. For now, let's assume she has simply invested £3,000 in cash into the business.

So, back to that other question. Why does the cash ledger show a debit balance when in fact the business has £3,000 in its bank account? The answer to this one is not so easy. Many accountancy teachers and books simply brush over this point and ask students to accept that it is the case. All ledgers which relate to assets (things that the business owns, including cash) will show additions as debits and deductions as credits. In many ways these teachers and books are right to ask you to simply accept the principle. It is an easy one to remember – the cash ledger works counter-intuitively, get used to it! If you want a more technical explanation, then think about it like this. The ledgers, or accounts, of a business could be said to be looking at things from the point of view of its owner. The £3,000 on the cash ledger is money which is potentially owed back to Abigail by the business as a debt. Alternatively, you could say that the various debit balances on the asset accounts reflect the use of the initial investment made by Abigail (her capital). However you look at it, there is no very easy explanation, and that is why many teachers and books ask you to accept it and move on. So let's do just that.

Abigail leaves the bank and heads off to the electronics shop on the high street. An hour later she buys a camera, a printer and some ink using the debit card that her bank has issued to her for her new business account. This gives rise to Abigail's second, third and fourth pair of accounting entries. Let's take each one in turn, starting with the purchase of the camera.

It is clear that in this transaction Abigail has spent some money. In fact, she paid £550 for the camera. She paid by debit card, but it is still recorded through the cash ledger. Here's what it will look like:

Cash

Date	Details	Dr	Cr	Balance
01/06	Capital	3000		3000dr
01/06	Cameras		550	2450dr

You will recall that the first entry (the £3,000) was already there from when she paid the cash into her business account. The second entry is the purchase of the camera. Abigail has spent £550 on the camera. Remember also that the cash ledger works in the opposite way to how you would expect it to operate, so that money going out of the ledger is in fact shown as a credit entry. The £550 has therefore been credited to the cash ledger, signifying that money has left the bank account. The balance on the ledger has consequently fallen to £2,450 debit, which means that Abigail's business now has £2,450 in its bank account.

The other side of the entry goes to her cameras ledger. That ledger records the value of the camera equipment that she owns. At the moment, that should show a balance of £550. This is what it will look like:

Cameras

Date	Details	Dr	Cr	Balance
01/06	Cash	550		550dr

Have you noticed the 'Details' column? Traditionally, this always begins with the name of the account in which the other side of the transaction has been recorded. In this case, it was the cash account. On the cash account entry, it states the details as 'Cameras'. This system allows anyone who needs to look at the books of account to trace the entries through and 'pair them up'. It aids understanding and interpretation of the accounts later. It also helps to find errors that might result in the ledgers not 'balancing', but we'll come back to that later.

Abigail also bought a printer using her debit card and the entries for that transaction will be the same as for the camera, except they will show in a 'Printers' ledger, rather than in the 'Cameras' ledger.

Assuming the printer cost £150, the entries would look like this:

Cash

Date	Details	Dr	Cr	Balance
01/06	Capital	3000		3000dr
01/06	Cameras		550	2450dr
01/06	Printers		150	2300dr

Printers

Date	Details	Dr	Cr	Balance
01/06	Cash	150		150dr

You might be asking yourself how we know what to call each ledger. Well, the answer is that some ledgers have traditional names which generally should be used by all businesses, such as 'Capital' and 'Cash'. We'll come across more as we go through the book. For others, you can, to some extent, make it up as you go along! For Abigail, we have chosen to have a 'Cameras' ledger and a 'Printers' ledger. Soon, we'll have a 'Computers' ledger for her too. But there is no reason why she couldn't have an 'Electronic Equipment' ledger, and put all three into one ledger. This is perhaps easier and keeps the number of accounts to a minimum. On the other hand, it would potentially provide less detail about her transactions. There are pros and cons to each, but for now, let's stick with what we have done so far and have a ledger for each type of item.

Abigail's camera and printer are known as 'assets' of the business. An asset is something which is owned by the business and generally has some value to it. Individual people also own assets. Some people are lucky enough to own a house. Many people own a car. Most people own other assets like clothes, books, electronic equipment and so on. The opposite of an asset is a liability. A liability is something that someone owes to someone else. A person with a bank loan has a liability. The size of that liability is equal to the amount outstanding on the loan. The loan is owed to someone else, in that case to the bank. We'll come back to liabilities later.

The final item that Abigail bought was some ink for her printer. This could be treated as another asset and we could start an 'Ink' ledger. However, ink is a little like other bits of stationery. No doubt Abigail will use folders, paper, pens and pencils, staples, sticky notes and so on in her business. She will probably get through these things quite quickly.

Due to the many things that make up 'stationery' and the speed at which the items come and go, many businesses treat it as an expense rather than record every item as individual assets. An expense is generally a payment made by the business which recurs to some degree. Obvious examples include rent, utility bills, wages paid to staff of the business, insurance costs and so on.

Let's treat Abigail's stationery as an expense. In fact, it makes little difference to the initial accounting entries, which would look like this (assuming she spent £50 on ink):

Cash

Date	Details	Dr	Cr	Balance
01/06	Capital	3000		3000dr
01/06	Cameras		550	2450dr
01/06	Printers		150	2300dr
01/06	Stationery		50	2250dr

Stationery

Date	Details	Dr	Cr	Balance
01/06	Cash	50		50dr

It is entirely acceptable to add more information in the "Details" column after the name of the ledger. So, in the Stationery ledger, we could write "Cash – Ink" to enable better records to be kept about what the stationery expense had been incurred on. Again, for now, let's keep it simple.

Notice that expense accounts tend to have a debit balance. This reflects the fact that they are a cost to the business and have resulted in a reduction in the assets of the business (usually its cash). Cash is an asset of the business because it is something which the business owns. The debit in an expense account is often paired with a credit in the cash account (which, remember, signifies a reduction in cash).

There's one more asset purchase transaction I want to consider here. Let's assume Abigail buys a laptop computer for her business on 2 June, but this time we'll assume that she pays for it on credit rather than by cash or debit card. In other words, she takes the computer away today, but agrees to pay for it later. Abigail finds a laptop which costs £900. She gets a good interest free deal and is required to pay £75 per month for the next 12 months (£900 in total). Let's see how we enter the initial purchase in her accounts.

First of all, we need to consider the nature of the credit transaction. Abigail did not pay anything *in cash* for the laptop at the time she actually bought it. That means there will be no movement on her cash ledger. She has made no withdrawal from her business bank account for the laptop; she didn't take cash out and she didn't use her debit card. She has paid nothing yet. We therefore do not need to make any entries on her cash ledger.

For now then, let's deal with the other side of the transaction, with which we are already familiar. That will go into the 'Computers' ledger as follows:

Computers

Date	Details	Dr	Cr	Balance
02/06	Cyril's Computers	900		900dr

As we have seen for other assets, this account reflects the fact that Abigail now owns a computer

worth £900. In the Details column we would usually
expect to see the word 'Cash', which would tell us
that the other side of the entry had gone to the cash
account. However, in this case she didn't pay cash for
the computer; she bought it on credit terms. The
Details here tell us that the computer was bought on
credit from Cyril's Computers. This is the name of the
business to which Abigail now owes £900. The other
side of this entry will look like this:

Cyril's Computers

Date	Details	Dr	Cr	Balance
02/06	Computers		900	900cr

This account is shown with a credit balance
because Cyril's Computers is now a creditor of
Abigail's business. In other words, someone to whom
Abigail owes money. This is an example of a liability,
which we touched on earlier. Liabilities have credit
balances because the person to whom money is owed
is a creditor of the business. Such people will usually
have provided something of value to the business in
the past. In this case, Cyril's Computers provided
Abigail with a computer worth £900.

We'll come back to credit transactions later in
the book, but just in case you are wondering, when
Abigail makes her monthly payments of £75 to Cyril's
Computers, she will credit £75 to her cash ledger (to

show cash going out), reducing her cash balance, and she will show a debit of £75 in the Cyril's Computers ledger, showing that she has paid back some of the debt she owes to that business, reducing the credit balance on the account. When she has completed the 12 payments, which will be a total of £900, then her cash ledger will be £900 worse off in total, but Cyril's Computers will show a zero balance, indicating that Abigail no longer owes any money to that business. We'll look at the entries for this later in the book.

Before we try to balance Abigail's books, let's look at one final transaction. On 3 June Abigail receives her first piece of work. She takes photographs of a group of family members who in return agree to pay £400 for a selection of photographs. They pay her in cash the same day.

The receipt of cash must obviously be recorded in the cash ledger. As a receipt, it will show as a debit entry (remember, the Cash ledger doesn't work quite as you would expect).

Abigail's Cash ledger will therefore look like this:

Cash

Date	Details	Dr	Cr	Balance
01/06	Capital	3000		3000dr
01/06	Cameras		550	2450dr
01/06	Printers		150	2300dr
01/06	Stationery		50	2250dr
03/06	Income	400		2650dr

That is the first receipt of cash that the business has had since the initial £3,000 paid in by Abigail to start it up. It takes her balance back up to £2,650dr, which actually means that she has £2,650 in her account.

Another question that might have been floating through your mind so far is that of bank statements. Bank statements show debits and credits in the traditional way, with money paid into the bank account showing as a credit and money taken out showing as a debit. In other words, the bank statement that Abigail receives from her bank will, in effect, be a mirror image of her own cash ledger. Again, the explanation for this is rather complex, but if you view Abigail's bank account from the *bank's* perspective, then it works the other way round. When Abigail pays money into her bank account, then it creates a debt for the bank that it must at some point repay to Abigail. That is why it is shown as a credit on her bank statement; it makes her a creditor as far as the bank is concerned. Similarly, if she goes overdrawn, she will be a debtor to the bank, in that she would then owe them money – any amounts drawn out are therefore shown as debits on her statement.

Returning to Abigail's latest transaction, we can see that the Details column of her cash ledger reads, 'Income'. This is the name of the ledger which has been used to show receipts which the business takes for providing its service. The family who purchased Abigail's photographs have paid for her skill as a photographer, rather than the actual paper on which the photographs are printed. Abigail doesn't sell goods in the same way as a supermarket might; she sells a service. Money she receives is therefore recorded in a ledger called 'Income'. The name of this ledger will vary from business to business. Of course, many businesses actually have more than one source of income. For example, they might provide other services, or they might receive interest from the bank. In those cases, more than one ledger would be needed, and each would have a different name.

In Abigail's case, the Income ledger will look like this:

Income

Date	Details	Dr	Cr	Balance
03/06	Cash		400	400cr

As usual, the entry is equal and opposite to the other entry that we made for this transaction, in the cash ledger. That should keep the books balanced, which brings me nicely to the next thing I want to look at - the trial balance.

A trial balance is exactly what it says it is – a check to see if everything balances. It can be carried out at any time, but is particularly important just before the final accounts are produced. Final accounts, consisting of a profit and loss account and a balance sheet, are generally produced each year at the year-end (remember we talked about this earlier – Abigail started her business on 1 June XXX1, and set her year-end for a date one year later, on 31 May XXX2. She would certainly want to produce a trial balance on that date, but for now let's have a look at her current position on 3 June XXX1 (three days into her business venture).

So how do we produce a trial balance? Well, we simply take all the balances from all the individual ledgers of Abigail's accounts and add them up (or at least add up the credit balances; debit balances should be taken away of course). The result should be zero; the credits should equal the debits.

Here's what Abigail's trial balance looks like:

Trial Balance – Abigail Photography – 3 June XXX1

Ledger	Debit (£)	Credit (£)
Cash	2,650	
Income		400
Cameras	550	
Printers	150	
Stationery	50	
Computers	900	
Cyril's Computers		900
Capital		3,000
Totals	**4,300**	**4,300**

Great, it balances! The credits equal the debits - both add up to £4,300 and they therefore effectively cancel each other out. Can you see that all we have done is to lift the balances from the various ledgers that we drew up earlier on and listed them in the columns according to whether they were debit or credit balances? Easy! Of course, as the business continues to enter into more transactions, the scope for error increases. Later, we'll look at what to do if things don't balance out as planned.

There are just a couple more things I want to take you through before we finish this chapter. I appreciate we have covered a lot, but we will go back through everything bit by bit in the remainder of the book.

I mentioned earlier the final accounts, and said that they consist mainly of the profit and loss account, and the balance sheet. Let's look at what those things are and what they tell us now, by constructing the final accounts for Abigail's business. They would usually be done at the end of the year, after Abigail's first year of trading, but let's prepare them now, on 3 June XXX1, so that we can see how they work.

It is important to start with the profit and loss account. This is because the final 'profit' figure that is produced is then entered into the balance sheet. We therefore cannot complete the balance sheet until the profit and loss account has been finalised.

Okay, so that's the order in which we do things, but what *are* these things?

The profit and loss account does what it says it does. It calculates the profit (or loss) that the business made in the period covered by the account. At this point it is important to consider what we mean by profit. Again, we will come back to this later in the book, but profit is calculated as the income which the business earns in a period, less the expenses that it incurs. In Abigail's case, her income is the amount she received from the family photographs she took and sold for £400. Her only expense was for stationery (the ink for her printer) of £50. Her profit for the period 1 to 3 June XXX1 therefore seems to be £350. Note that this is not the same as the cash that the business owns. The business has £2,650 in cash;

this is not relevant to the calculation of her profit. Note also that the other assets (other than cash) that Abigail's business owns, such as the camera, printer and the computer, are also not taken into account when calculating her profit. Again, we'll think about why this is when we come back to look at things in more detail later in the book.

Let's set out Abigail's profit and loss account:

Profit and Loss Account for Abigail Photography for the period ending 3 June XXX1

	£	£
Income		400
Less: Expenses		
Stationery		(50)
Net Profit		**350**

And there we have it. Now, things *do* become more complex of course, but three days into Abigail's business venture, she has made a good profit. There are a few things to note about this profit and loss account however. First, thinking about the ink in her printer, presumably Abigail hasn't used it *all* in the period 1 to 3 June. In other words, *some* of the £50 spent on ink relates to ink used in the period 1 to 3 June (the period covered by the accounts). The remaining ink will be used in a later period. It is therefore inaccurate to say that her stationery expense for the period covered by the profit and loss account is £50. That is how much she *spent*, but not how much actually relates to that period. It would probably be more accurate to say that the cost of the ink for the period 1 to 3 June was £10, or £20, depending how much ink she has used for the one job that she has undertaken, and this is the figure that would actually be included here, not the full £50. This is called a 'prepayment'. It means that Abigail has spent money in one period, which actually relates (at least in part) to a later period. The expense should be spread across both periods to which it relates. Again, we'll deal with this in more detail later in the book, but we'll keep it simple and leave it at £50 for now.

Another thing to note is the use of brackets in the profit and loss account. In accountancy, this generally denotes that a number is being subtracted from another number. Here, the stationery cost of £50 (in brackets) has been deducted from the £400 income.

Finally, the term 'Net Profit' means the profit after expenses have been deducted - more on this later too.

Okay, let's move on to the final thing I want to look at for this chapter, and that is the balance sheet. The balance sheet has a top half and a bottom half, and these two parts should balance, hence the name.

The top half sets out the business's assets (things the business owns or which have some value in another sense) and liabilities (things the business owes to others).

The bottom half sets out the amount of capital that the owners of the business have invested, and this includes any profit that the business has made, since this too potentially belongs to the owners and certainly reflects an increase in the value of the business.

So let's have a think about Abigail's business. In terms of assets that it owns, if we look back to the trial balance, we can see that it owns a camera, a printer and a computer. Remember, we decided to treat the stationery (ink) as an expense and so this has already been dealt with in the profit and loss account above. The other thing of value is of course the cash.

In terms of liabilities, or things that the business owes to others, the most obvious entry is the amount owed to Cyril's Computers.

Okay, let's put the balance sheet together.

Balance Sheet for Abigail Photography as at 3 June XXX1

	£	£
Employment of Capital		
Fixed Assets:		
Camera		550
Computer		900
Printer		150
		1,600
Current Assets:		
Cash	2,650	
Current Liabilities:		
Cyril's Computers	(900)	
Net Current Assets		1,750
Net Assets		**3,350**
Capital Employed		
Capital	3,000	
Profit	350	**3,350**

Fortunately it balances! The balancing figure is £3,350. One thing that is worth noting is that each of the eight figures in the original trial balance has been used just once in constructing the profit and loss account and the balance sheet. Each item appears only once in either of these two statements. In this case, two of them appeared in the profit and loss account (Income and Stationery) and the other six appeared in the balance sheet (Camera, Computer, Printer, Cash, Cyril's Computers and Capital).

In the bottom half of the balance sheet you can see details of the 'capital employed'. This sets out the amount that Abigail has tied up in the business. We know she invested £3,000 to start up the business, and we can see that the profit she has made so far (the £350 shown in the profit and loss account earlier in this chapter) has been added to it to give the resulting £3,350.

The top half of the balance sheet is a little more complex and therefore requires more explanation. This part is headed up 'Employment of Capital'. In other words, it is showing exactly how the capital that Abigail has invested has been employed. We know her capital is £3,350 (her initial investment plus her profit to date). The top half of the balance sheet shows us how that £3,350 is being used in the business. The top half must obviously therefore also total £3,350, as indeed it does.

The first thing the balance sheet does is to set out the fixed assets of the business. A fixed asset is an asset which the business owns for use within the business. Abigail has bought a camera, a computer and a printer to use within her business. She hasn't purchased them with a view to selling them for a profit (in other words, for more than she bought them for). She is a photographer, and these assets are items she has acquired for long term use to help her run her photographer business. Abigail makes her money by selling her photography services. The camera, computer and printer are assets which remain in her business as she goes about doing that. They are fixed assets. It is unlikely that she will replace them within the next 12 months, which is a good general test as to whether something is a fixed asset.

We have listed her fixed assets and then added them up. The values used are the prices that she paid for the assets. Note that accounts should give a true and fair view of the financial position of the business. In actual fact, those assets will have lost some of their value as soon as Abigail bought them, and certainly after she used them. We will see later in the book that an adjustment can be made to reflect this loss in value (called depreciation) but for now, again we'll keep things simple and leave the values as they are.

Next, the balance sheet deals with current assets. These are assets which are cash, or are likely to be turned into cash, in the next 12 months. In this case, just the cash is included, but we'll cover more items which could be listed here later in the book.

Before we add the current assets to the fixed assets, you will see that the balance sheet first lists the current liabilities and deducts them from the current assets. This is because current liabilities are things which the business is likely to need to pay out within the next 12 months. It is therefore useful to compare them to the amounts which the business already has (cash) or are likely to be turned into cash in the same period (other current assets). In this case we can clearly see that Abigail has enough cash (£2,650) to pay the outstanding liability to Cyril's Computers (£900) as and when it falls due. This is important, because a business which cannot pay its debts as they fall due might be insolvent, which means it might run into financial difficulties in the near future, if it hasn't already done so.

Having deducted the current liabilities from the Current assets, we can then add the net result (the 'Net Current Assets') to Abigail's fixed assets to establish the total capital that has been employed. As stated earlier, this must equal the capital that Abigail now has invested in the business.

The resulting figure of £3,350 is also a very basic method of valuing a business. The top half of the balance sheet has listed the values of the assets and liabilities in Abigail's business. At a basic level, we could say that if she finished in business today, she could sell her fixed assets for the values stated, add it to her cash and pay the debt owed to Cyril's Computers. If she did this, then she would have £3,350 left over. Therefore, that is the value that she should look to sell her business for. There are, of course many factors that have an effect on this valuation. We've already said that the fixed assets in Abigail's business are not going to be worth the values stated due to depreciation. Also, once Abigail's business is fully up and running, it might have a reputation that is worth something; the name in itself might be one people relate to, and she might have a list of repeat customers who return to her for her services on a regular basis, and who recommend her work to others. These factors alone mean that the business may actually be worth less (due to depreciation) or more (due to her reputation) than simply the value of the assets and liabilities listed in the balance sheet.

I propose to leave this chapter here. I want to assure you that we will revisit everything we've covered so far again at some point in this book. I hope you've found this chapter interesting and useful in giving you an overview and a foundation on which to build.

Chapter 3 – Profit, Turnover and Cash

In this chapter I want to cover three business terms which are often confused with each other. Those new to accountancy often think that profit, turnover and cash are terms which are interchangeable; that they mean the same thing. However, that is far from true; they each have their own specific meaning, and it is essential for a good understanding of accountancy generally that you are clear on the differences between them. This chapter aims to make sure that you are.

Here is a basic explanation of what each of those three terms means.

'Profit' is found by adding up the income of a business for a certain period and then deducting any related expenses. It measures the gap between the two. Hopefully income will exceed expenses, which will result in a profit. If expenses exceed income, then a loss will be made (effectively a negative profit, if you like). We have already seen this 'income minus expenses' calculation in operation in the profit and loss account which we drew up for Abigail's business in the previous chapter; that statement set out her income from her photography business and then deducted any related expenses to give her profit.

'Turnover' on the other hand, is the amount of money that passes into the business. It simply measures the amount of money from sales in the period. An increase in turnover *may* lead to an increase in profit, but not necessarily. Of course, if expenses increase by more than the increase in turnover, then there will actually be a decrease in profit.

'Cash' is the most basic of the definitions. As we have already seen in the previous chapter, cash simply means the money held by the business, usually at the bank. Again, a higher level of cash *may* mean a higher profit, but this is not necessarily the case.

I suspect an example will help to cement the differences between the three terms, so let's have a look at one now.

Bailey runs a retail business which sells laptops and related accessories. If he sells a laptop for £400 then his turnover on that sale is £400; that is the amount of money due to his business on that sale. If he sells ten laptops in a month, then his turnover for the month will be £4,000. This tells us nothing about his profit, only about his sale price and volume of sales. Of course, it is still a useful measure. If he increases his price to £450, but his sales only drop by one laptop, so that he sells nine laptops the next month, his turnover will now be £4,050. That would suggest that it is worthwhile increasing his prices, as the resulting drop in demand is not enough to result in an overall drop in turnover; more money will come into the business. If he increases his prices to £500 and sales drop to seven laptops, then his overall turnover for the month has dropped to £3,500, suggesting that he has overpriced his products.

Let's assume that each laptop costs Bailey £250 in total. That includes the actual cost of buying the laptop and a proportion of all related expenses, such as rent on his small shop, insurance, utility bills and so on. If Bailey sells one laptop for £400, then as we have seen, his turnover is £400, being the amount he receives for the laptop. However, his profit will be £150 on that sale. This is the income received from it (£400) less expenses (£250). If he sells ten laptops in a month, then his profit will be £1,500 (10 x £150). His turnover for those same ten sales will be £4,000 as discussed above (10 x £400).

In terms of cash, let's keep it simple (if not entirely realistic) and assume that he started his business with £2,500 cash, which he then spent in order to buy the ten laptops at £250 each. Now that he has sold them all, he will have £4,000 in the bank, assuming his customers all paid the £400 sale price in cash.

So we can see that Bailey had a monthly turnover of £4,000, cash of £4,000 and a total profit of £1,500. There has been some correlation between the three figures (especially turnover and cash), but that will not always be the case. Let's look at an alternative scenario for Bailey.

Let's assume this time that five of the ten computers that he sells are sold on credit. That means that his customers do not pay up front in cash, but have agreed to pay at some point in the future, perhaps in monthly instalments. Bailey's turnover will still be £4,000 for the month, because turnover includes the value of all sales made by the business, not just those that have been paid for in cash. Similarly, his profit will still be £1,500, as again this figure includes items which have been sold but not yet paid for. However, his cash balance will be lower. The five customers who *have* paid will have paid £2,000 in total. The other £2,000 is still outstanding from the other five credit buyers.

Another factor to consider in all this is the cost of the laptops to Bailey. We said he pays £250 for each laptop. But what if this figure increases? If it goes up to £300, then suddenly he is only making £100 profit on each sale rather than the £150 that he was making previously. However, his turnover on each sale would remain at £400, as this is what he is selling them for. His monthly profit from the sale of ten laptops would therefore be £1,000, rather than £1,500. Of course, he may choose to increase his selling price to maintain his profit level, but that rather depends on whether his customers will be prepared to pay the increased prices.

And in terms of cash, Bailey may of course decide to spend some of his cash on fixed assets. We saw in the previous chapter that a fixed asset is something which a business buys with a view to keeping and using it within the business. If he buys a delivery van for £1,200, then his cash will fall by that amount, but it won't affect his profit or turnover levels. If we think back to the balance sheet for Abigail, we saw that both fixed assets and current assets (assets which are cash, or likely to be turned into cash in the next 12 months) appeared on that statement. By spending cash (a current asset) on a van (a fixed asset), all we are doing is adjusting the assets of the business - redistributing the values if you like. It will result in a decrease in current assets and an increase in fixed assets. Profit levels are not directly affected by this. Profit is only affected by a change in income or a change in expenses. Buying a van is not in itself an expense because the value of the cash lost has simply been replaced by the value of the van.

Hopefully this chapter has helped you to appreciate the difference between turnover, profit and cash. As ever, we'll return to these concepts as we go on, so don't worry if things are not quite clear yet – it'll come!

Chapter 4 – Assets and Liabilities (not Stock)

In this chapter I want to return to something we have talked about several times already – assets and liabilities. Stock is also an asset, but we'll deal with that in the next chapter. Remember, an asset is something which a business owns; it generally has some kind of value to the business. A liability, on the other hand, is something the business owes to someone else. They both appear in the accounts on the balance sheet, which is effectively a list of assets and liabilities.

It is important to be clear that an asset is generally owned by the business, not borrowed or in some other way temporarily available to it. An example of what I mean by this can be seen in relation to land and buildings. If a business owns the premises from which it operates, then those premises will be an asset and will appear on the balance sheet of the business. However, if the business rents the premises from a landlord, as many businesses do, then the business does not own the premises, it merely has temporary rights over the land, including the right of occupation, granted by the landlord in return for the payment of rent. In that case, the premises will not appear on the balance sheet of the business. The rent payable for use of the premises is actually an expense, which will appear on the profit and loss account, directly reducing the profit made by the business. If that rent falls into arrears or is for some other reason unpaid, then the unpaid element will be a liability – something owed by the business. Another example would be a van which is owned (an asset) and a van which is leased (where the lease payments would be an expense, or a liability if left unpaid). It is in this sense that we sometimes talk about rent as 'dead money' – it is paid out to someone else and lost for good. No asset is received in return as it is when premises are purchased. It leads to an expense that reduces the profit of the business. On a purchase, the money paid out is replaced by the receipt of another asset (the thing purchased) and therefore gives rise to no expense as such.

Before we remind ourselves of exactly how to deal with assets and liabilities in the accounts, let's make sure we are happy with the distinction between fixed assets and current assets (which we have looked at before), and between current liabilities and long term liabilities (which is new to us).

A fixed asset is generally something that a business buys with a view to keeping it within the business and using it in some way. Common examples include land and buildings, fixtures and fittings, machinery, motor vehicles, computers and other equipment. We could also label these assets as 'tangible' assets. This means that we can reach out and touch them – they are real, actual objects. An intangible asset, on the other hand, is still something that a business owns, but generally not something that we can grab hold of! For example, the ownership of a copyright or patent may well be worth something in monetary terms, but it is a right, rather than an object. However, it is still a fixed asset, the value of which we can record in the balance sheet. Some types of long term investments that a business might make are another example of an intangible fixed asset. Detail on this is beyond the scope of an introductory book of this nature.

A current asset, on the other hand, is something which is either cash, or likely to be turned into cash in the next 12 months. Common examples include cash itself, obviously, but also the stock of the business, which hopefully will be sold fairly soon (we'll look at this in more detail in the next chapter). Current assets can be intangible too, and debts owed to the business are an example of this. If a business allows a customer to buy something on credit (that is, take it away now but pay for it later) then the debt owed by the customer becomes a 'book debt' which is an intangible current asset. It is something of value to the business, but not something we can reach out and touch. However, when it comes to the balance sheet, intangible current assets are not separately identified and so the distinction is less important than it is with fixed assets.

When it comes to liabilities, the position is similar. A current liability is a liability that is likely to fall due within the next 12 months. We saw earlier the example of an outstanding trade creditor. If a business buys goods for its trade and agrees with the seller to take the goods now but pay for them later, then the outstanding amount is called 'credit'. It is something that the business owes to someone else. It is therefore a liability and, as it is likely to be due in the next 12 months, then it is a current liability. Other common current liabilities include expenses which are due but not yet paid as explained above (often referred to as accruals), and any bank overdraft (in other words, where the cash ledger goes 'overdrawn' or into the red).

A long term liability is therefore a liability which is likely to be due in more than 12 months' time. The most common example is longer term bank finance such as a bank loan, which may often be taken out over a term of several years.

When dealing with the assets and liabilities of a business in the accounts, we saw earlier that they generally appear on the balance sheet. Remember that the balance sheet is really just a list of the assets and liabilities of a business. Fixed assets are generally listed first, followed by current assets, and then current liabilities, and finally long term liabilities.

The initial accounting entries in the double entry ledgers for assets follow the same rules as for cash (which is, of course, an asset in itself). In other words, we debit the asset account when new assets are bought, and credit them when they are sold or in some other way disposed of. We can remind ourselves here that the cash ledger seemed to work counter-intuitively, in that when cash was received we debited the cash ledger, and when it was paid out it was credited; we discussed a few rationales for this and decided, in the end, simply to accept the rule. Generally then, we can say that when an asset increases (cash received or some other asset acquired) we debit the relevant account, and when as asset reduces (cash paid out or some other asset disposed of) we credit the relevant account.

For liabilities, the rules are basically the same as they are for assets, but opposite. If a business pays a creditor in cash then we would, as expected, credit the cash ledger to signify the reduction in cash (an asset). The creditor's ledger, on the other hand, would be debited, which would have the effect of extinguishing the credit provided by that creditor. In other words, the reduction in the liability has been reflected by a debit entry. This is, of course, the opposite of how assets work. We have said that assets are debited when they *increase*. As liabilities are in themselves the opposite of assets, then it must be the case that the rules, whilst similar, work in the opposite way. In other words, an increase in a liability is shown by a credit entry, whilst a reduction is shown by a debit entry.

Another example might help. If a business borrows money from a bank, then its cash will increase, so we would debit the cash ledger. The credit entry would then be made in the 'bank loans' ledger (or similar) which will have the effect of increasing the credit (or funding) provided by the bank. Again, we can see here that an increase in a liability (the bank loan) is shown by a credit entry in the relevant ledger. The bank has become a creditor to the business – it has provided credit.

We'll remind ourselves of some examples shortly, but there is something else that is quite useful to recognise here. A reduction in one asset often leads to the increase in another and vice versa. In other words, the value in the business is simply being shifted from one class of assets to another. For example, if a business buys a new van for cash, the reduction in one asset (cash) is 'balanced' by the increase in another asset (motor vehicles). This also works when we factor in liabilities.

If a business buys some furniture on credit, then the increase in one asset, furniture, is offset by the increase in a liability, being the credit provided to the business by the furniture supplier. The balance sheet shows assets less liabilities, so that in this case the overall position remains the same. Assets have been increased, but so have liabilities by the same amount. The balance sheet remains balanced.

Of course, knowing what we now know about assets and liabilities, it kind of begs the question as to how a profit is made. If a business is simply shifting value around amongst its assets and liabilities, then at what point does a business actually create a profit?

The answer lies in the notion of stock, which we'll look at in the next chapter, income, which we considered earlier for Abigail, and also in expenses, which we'll consider later in the book. A trading business buys stock and sells it at a higher price, creating gross profit. A service provider (like Abigail the photographer) provides a service for which they charge a fee. As long as the gross profit, or fee, exceeds the related expenses then an overall (or net) profit will arise.

Before we finish this chapter, let's remind ourselves of the basic accounting entries for assets and liabilities, together with some new entries. To do this, we'll consider Andrew's business. Andrew supplies domestic electrical products from a small shop he rents. He is looking to replace his rather dilapidated delivery van, and has arranged a bank loan to do this.

Today, which we will say is 10 May, Andrew is overdrawn at the bank, and his cash ledger reflects this position. It looks like this:

Cash

Date	Details	Dr	Cr	Balance
10/05	Balance forward			800cr

There have of course been many previous transactions through his cash ledger, but I have not shown these as they are not relevant. All that is relevant is the current balance, which is £800 overdrawn. Remember, the cash ledger operates counter-intuitively, so that a credit balance actually means the ledger is in the red (overdrawn).

Andrew's bank agrees to lend him £6,000 to purchase a second hand delivery van. The injection of cash from the bank will lead to a debit in Andrew's cash ledger (of course, at the bank itself, his actual bank account will have £6,000 deposited into it). The ledger will therefore go from being £800 overdrawn, to £5,200 in the black.

It will look like this:

Cash

Date	Details	Dr	Cr	Balance
10/05	Balance forward			800cr
10/05	Bank loan	6000		5200dr

Andrew now has £5,200 in his cash ledger to spend on a new van and, assuming his bank is still happy for him to run an overdraft of £800, he could actually spend up to £6,000 on the replacement van.

The other side of this double entry transaction will create a liability. Here it is:

Bank Loan

Date	Details	Dr	Cr	Balance
10/05	Cash		6000	6000cr

The increase in the asset (cash) has been offset by an increase in a liability (the loan). The value of the business as a whole is basically unaffected. In theory, Andrew could repay the loan now, using £6,000 in cash, which would reverse out the above entries. Of course, he won't do that, because he intends to buy a replacement van. Let's assume he buys a van a couple of days later for £5,900, and remind ourselves of how that will show in his accounts. Firstly, the cash ledger:

Cash

Date	Details	Dr	Cr	Balance
10/05	Balance forward			800cr
10/05	Bank Loan	6000		5200dr
12/05	Motor Vehicles		5900	700cr

And now the Motor Vehicles ledger:

Motor Vehicles

Date	Details	Dr	Cr	Balance
12/05	Cash	5900		5900dr

This time an increase in one asset (motor vehicles) has been offset by a decrease in another asset (cash). Once again the overall value of the business remains roughly the same. All that has happened is that £5,900 in cash has been replaced by a van which is worth around £5,900.

These two transactions have required the use of three ledgers. When it comes to producing the balance sheet, the Motor Vehicles ledger will appear as a fixed asset, the cash ledger as a current asset and the bank loan as a liability, probably a long term liability depending on exactly what has been agreed with the bank in terms of its duration.

Just to complete the cycle, let's have a quick look at what happens when Andrew makes his first loan repayment. Assuming he pays £200 back every month, then his first payment will be due on 10 June. When he makes that payment, Andrew's cash ledger will show a credit (reduction) of £200 and his bank loan will show a debit (also a reduction, because liabilities work in the opposite way to assets) for the same amount. Here they are:

Cash

Date	Details	Dr	Cr	Balance
10/05	Balance forward			800cr
10/05	Bank Loan	6000		5200dr
12/05	Motor Vehicles		5900	700cr
10/06	Bank Loan		200	900cr

Bank Loan

Date	Details	Dr	Cr	Balance
10/05	Cash		6000	6000cr
10/06	Cash	200		5800cr

The decrease in the cash ledger is offset by a corresponding decrease in the bank loan ledger. Of course, in actual fact Andrew will have to pay some interest on his loan, which will be an expense for his business, having a direct impact on his profit, but we'll come back to that when we look in more detail at expenses later in the book.

This chapter has looked a little more at assets and liabilities. One important asset has been deliberately overlooked for now, which is stock, and it is to stock that we now need to turn our attention.

Chapter 5 – Stock (and Work in Progress)

We have seen previously that stock is an example of a current asset of a business. It is crucial to understand what is meant by stock in order to get a true understanding of accountancy in general. The stock of a business is the collection of assets which that business buys and sells with a view to making a profit. In order to identify the stock, it is therefore necessary to identify what type of business is being run. The following two examples should help.

A supermarket has, as its stock, all the food and other items which are for sale in its stores, together with items in storage or in transport which it owns.

A shoe shop has, as its stock, all the shoes, trainers, boots, slippers and other items it has for sale in its shop, again together with similar items in storage or in the process of being transported.

These two businesses provide pretty straightforward examples. It is reasonably easy to identify the stock, and therefore also to identify what is *not* stock, which is just as important when drawing up the accounts. A supermarket clearly owns a lot more assets than just its stock (as indeed might a shoe shop). For example, it might own the buildings in which its stores are located. It probably owns some vehicles, and it almost certainly owns things like shelving and computer systems. However, these other assets are not stock; the supermarket does not own them with a view to selling them on for a profit. So whilst all assets appear on the balance sheet, those items which are included within the term 'stock' need to be identified with care.

Of course, what constitutes stock in one business might not constitute stock in another. For example, we have seen that a shop might own the shelving on which it displays its stock for customers to see. The shelving itself is therefore not stock, as it is not in itself for sale. However, consider the business which supplies that shelving in the first place. For *that* business, shelving is its stock. It buys shelving from a shelving manufacturer (let's say) and sells it on for a profit to shops who want to use it to display their own stock. The stock of shelving that this shelving business has to sell to those shops therefore constitutes the stock of the shelving business, and it will appear in the accounts as 'stock', rather than as a fixed asset under 'shelving' or 'shop furniture' or similar (as it would for most other businesses).

Another example might be a business that sells computers. Its stock will consist of a range of computer hardware, accessories and probably software too. However, when it sells one of those computers to another business, that computer is likely to become a fixed asset for that other business, which probably intends to use the computer within its business rather than sell it on for profit. For example, a photographer like Abigail, who we met earlier in the book, bought a computer for the storage and alteration of photographs. In that case the computer was a fixed asset, not stock. In fact, Abigail didn't really have any stock at all, because what she really provided was a service – a photography service, not goods, but we'll deal with this point in more detail later.

The importance of being able to identify which assets constitute the stock of a business comes to the fore when we look at how stock is recorded in the accounts of a business. The first thing to note is that there is no 'Stock' ledger. Instead, we record sales and purchases of stock separately in two ledgers with those names. Let's look at an example.

Alice started in business on 1 April by opening a small gift shop in a small town on the coast. She invested £5,000 of her savings into the business. She has bought a cash register and some basic shelving which cost £1,000. Remember, these things are fixed assets, as she does not intend to sell them; they are for use within the business. She now wants to buy some stock to fill her shop. Having visited a local wholesaler which specialises in gift items, she has now started to fill her shelving with attractive items typically sold in coastal gift shops. In total, she spent £2,500 on her initial stock.

After the purchase of the stock, her cash ledger will look like this:

Cash

Date	Details	Dr	Cr	Balance
01/04	Capital	5000		5000dr
01/04	Fixtures & Fittings		1000	4000dr
01/04	Purchases		2500	1500dr

Alice's initial capital investment is a useful reminder of what we looked at earlier when Abigail started her photography business. This entry reflects the fact that Alice has paid £5,000 of her own money into the business. This investment is referred to as the owner's capital. Just as a reminder, the capital ledger (in which the other side of this entry would have been made) would look like this:

Capital

Date	Details	Dr	Cr	Balance
01/04	Cash		5000	5000cr

The cash register and the shelving have been grouped together and entered into the cash ledger as 'Fixtures & Fittings'. The other side of this entry would of course be entered (as a debit) in the usual way into an asset ledger called 'Fixtures & Fittings':

Fixtures & Fittings

Date	Details	Dr	Cr	Balance
01/04	Cash	1000		1000dr

That brings us to the final entry in Alice's cash ledger – the purchases. We said earlier that there is no 'Stock' ledger. So far, Alice has purchased stock (from the wholesaler) and this purchase is recorded in a purchases ledger as follows:

Purchases

Date	Details	Dr	Cr	Balance
01/04	Cash	2500		2500dr

Note that this ledger is only for purchases of stock, not other assets. It tells us nothing else other than that Alice has purchased £2,500 worth of stock. It does not tell us anything about the actual physical quantity of stock that has been purchased. If she visits the wholesaler again next month and buys another £2,500 worth of stock, she might of course get more or less for her money. That depends on whether the prices charged by the wholesaler have gone up or down in the interim period.

So we have seen what happens when Alice buys her stock. But what happens when she sells it?

The answer is that the entries are recorded in a Sales ledger.

Let's assume that Alice opens her shop for business on 2 April and during that day she sells stock to the value of £200. Assuming these were cash sales, then her business will have received £200 in cash. We can therefore add this entry to her growing cash ledger:

Cash

Date	Details	Dr	Cr	Balance
01/04	Capital	5000		5000dr
01/04	Fixtures & Fittings		1000	4000dr
01/04	Purchases		2500	1500dr
02/04	Sales	200		1700dr

It goes in as a debit entry of course as it is increasing an asset (cash). Her balance therefore grows from £1,500 to £1,700. The other side of the entry goes into her sales ledger as follows:

Sales

Date	Details	Dr	Cr	Balance
02/04	Cash		200	200cr

This ledger will have entries added to it each time Alice makes some Sales. If she is updating the accounts manually, then she might well simply total each day's sales and make the entry like we have done above. If her accounts are automated and linked to her cash register, then each and every sale may be individually recorded by the computer.

Again it is important to note that this ledger deals with monetary value and not physical quantities. The sales ledger does not tell us what was sold or how many, only the monetary amount of those sales. Of course, Alice will hope that she is selling her stock to the public for more than she paid for it at the wholesalers. If she does that, then she will be making a profit, or at least a gross profit (before deduction of her expenses).

After several months which will involve dozens of days' worth of sales and probably a couple more visits to the wholesaler to stock up the emptying shelves, the sales and purchases ledgers will have many entries in them, and the problem of identifying the actual stock in the business is magnified. The ledgers will list the amounts paid for purchases and the amounts charged for sales, but they do not tell us how much stock is in the shop.

Obviously, Alice can simply look around her shop to determine whether she thinks she needs more stock or not, but sometimes we need a more scientific way of dealing with this. You will recall earlier in the book when we talked about a trial balance...

You don't?

Well let me remind you. We said a trial balance was simply a list of the balances on all the ledgers. Because the sales and purchases ledgers are part of the double entry bookkeeping process, the trial balance will include these two ledgers and it should of course still balance. However, when we go further and draw up the final accounts – the profit and loss account and the balance sheet – we will need to ascertain a precise figure for the value of the stock in Alice's shop. And that is where the stocktake comes in.

A stocktake requires Alice to make a detailed record of every item of stock in her business and then attribute a value to it. Accounting principles tell us that this stock should be valued at the *lower* of its acquisition cost or its realisable value. In other words, Alice should start on the basis that it is worth what she paid for it, and then consider whether that is actually the case. If for some reason it has lost value, perhaps because it is damaged or because it is now out of fashion or obsolete, then she should value it at the price which she could realistically sell it for. Hence, she must value her stock at the *lower* of the acquisition cost, or its realisable value. The rationale behind this is that when producing accounts, they must show a true and fair view of the financial position of the business, and if there is any doubt, then we should be prudent in our estimations. Note in the case of stock the one thing we cannot do is value it in our accounts at its *selling price*, which will almost certainly be higher than the acquisition cost. The selling price of stock tends to be higher than the acquisition price because that is how businesses make their profit. We are not saying that Alice will not sell any of her stock at the prices she has it for sale at in her shop, but until she does, she can only value that unsold stock at the price she paid for it (or a lower price if that is more realistic).

So we have seen in this chapter that a business which buys and sells stock will need to record the purchases of stock in a purchases ledger and the sales in a sales ledger. These ledgers will allow us to work out the profit which the business has made. This is done as part of drawing up the profit and loss account, which we looked at earlier, but to which we will return in more detail later.

Before we leave this chapter, I just want to have another think back to Abigail and her photography business. We said at the time that she provided a service, that service being photography. She didn't buy and sell goods like Alice does in her gift shop. When Abigail made a 'sale' of her services, we therefore did not record this in a sales ledger, but rather we entered it into a ledger called 'income'. This serves the same purpose as the sales ledger in many respects, in that it records the turnover of the business (how much money comes in from the main business operation). However, for Abigail the photographer, there will be no purchases ledger because she does not purchase any stock. So we can see a difference here between traders, like Alice and her gift shop, and service providers, like Abigail.

Another difference is that because Abigail has no stock, she will instead have something called 'work in progress'. Work in progress is work which Abigail has undertaken but for which she has not yet billed her client. For example, she might have taken a range of photographs and edited them, but not yet printed them out and sent a bill to her client. The work she has done so far has some value, and Abigail can include it as a current asset on her balance sheet. It will also have an effect on her profit levels in her profit and loss account, but again we'll look at this later on. Abigail will value her work in progress by considering what she can charge the client for the final work, and then apply a completion percentage based on how much of it she has done. Valuing work in progress is in fact a complex task and the finer details are beyond the scope of an introductory book of this nature.

Chapter 6 – Credit Sales and Credit Purchases

Now that we have seen how the sales and purchases ledgers work, it is worth taking a moment to think about sales and purchases which are made on credit. Thinking back to Abigail's photography business, we saw how she bought a computer on credit from Cyril's Computers. This was the purchase of an asset. What we are going to consider in this chapter is similar, but we are going to look at trade transactions on credit. In other words, sales and purchases of stock where no cash is paid up front, but rather it is paid, by agreement, in the future.

Let me introduce you to Mary, who runs a second hand car business. She buys and sells cars, which means that for her, cars are her stock. When she buys cars, she records them in a purchases ledger, and when she sells them, she records them in a sales ledger.

But what if she buys a car on credit? Let's assume that a good source of cars for her business come from the major car dealer down the road. That business sells brand new cars and its own customers often part exchange their existing cars for a new car. The new car dealer then sells those second hand cars that it receives to Mary. It allows Mary to pay for them over a six month period.

When Mary purchases a car from the dealer for say, £2,400, she will record it in her purchases ledger as follows:

Purchases

Date	Details	Dr	Cr	Balance
04/12	Car Dealer	2400		2400dr

There's not much that is new here – we've simply debited the purchases ledger as usual. If she had bought it for cash then we'd expect a credit to the cash ledger for the same amount. However, she hasn't spent any cash yet, as she is allowed to pay for this stock over the next six months. Mary therefore needs to record the car dealer as a creditor (someone to whom she owes money) as follows:

Car Dealer

Date	Details	Dr	Cr	Balance
04/12	Purchases		2400	2400cr

If Mary was to draw up a balance sheet now, then the car dealer ledger would be included under 'Creditors' on the balance sheet as a current liability (due in the next 12 months).

When Mary makes her first monthly payment, this *will* be reflected in her cash ledger, because it involves a movement of cash. It will also be recorded in the car dealer ledger, reducing the amount owed to them. Here is that entry:

Car Dealer

Date	Details	Dr	Cr	Balance
04/12	Purchases		2400	2400cr
04/01	Cash	400		2000cr

This continues until Mary pays off the amount due (six monthly instalments of £400 each gives £2400).

The same process applies to sales that Mary makes on credit to her own customers, except these are recorded in the sales ledger and result in the creation of debtors (who owe her money) rather than creditors (to whom she owes money).

Let's assume she sells a car on credit for £3,600 and allows her customer to pay in 12 equal monthly instalments of £300.

When she makes the sale she will record it in her sales ledger as follows:

Sales

Date	Details	Dr	Cr	Balance
13/12	John Smith		3600	3600cr

Again the sale is recorded as expected in the sales ledger, but rather than a cash entry, we can see that the other side of the transaction will be recorded in John Smith's ledger (the name of the customer). That will look like this:

John Smith

Date	Details	Dr	Cr	Balance
13/12	Sales	3600		3600dr

If Mary draws up a balance sheet now, this debt would appear as part of her 'Debtors' as a current asset.

And again, when John Smith makes his first payment, the £300 would be debited in the usual way to Mary's cash ledger (to show the receipt) and John Smith's ledger will be credited to show a reduction in the debt which he owes to her. It will look like this:

John Smith

Date	Details	Dr	Cr	Balance
13/12	Sales	3600		3600dr
13/01	Cash		300	3300dr

If we forward-wind 12 months, to when he has paid off the debt completely, the ledger can effectively be closed off as the balance will be zero. It would look like this:

John Smith

Date	Details	Dr	Cr	Balance
13/12	Sales	3600		3600dr
13/01	Cash		300	3300dr
13/02	Cash		300	3000dr
13/03	Cash		300	2700dr
13/04	Cash		300	2400dr
13/05	Cash		300	2100dr
13/06	Cash		300	1800dr
13/07	Cash		300	1500dr
13/08	Cash		300	1200dr
13/09	Cash		300	900dr
13/10	Cash		300	600dr
13/11	Cash		300	300dr
13/12	Cash		300	0

Chapter 7 – Expenses

So far we have only briefly touched on the concept of an expense. When we looked at Abigail's photography business, we saw that her purchase of ink for her printer could be classified as an expense. Other common expenses include the payment of wages and salaries, the payment of bills such as utility bills, business rates and telephone bills, payments of rent and other property related expenses, as well as the cost of insurance. The list goes on and on, and each business is likely to have some expenses which are particular to that business. A car dealer, for example, might have the expense of cleaning products to keep the cars clean (or car wash fees).

So how do we identify an expense? And in particular, how do we differentiate it from money spent on acquiring assets?

The first thing is to remember that an asset is generally something that is purchased for use within the business in some way. Fixed assets are purchased to be used in the long term interests of the business, and can include property, machinery, vehicles and so on. Current assets, or at least stock, is bought with a view to it being sold for a profit in the relatively short term. Fixed assets tend to be 'one-off' purchases, whilst stock is a more regular purchase (at least, for most businesses).

The first feature of an expense is that they also tend to be regular, or repeating, payments. Think of the examples given at the start of this chapter. Salaries, bills and other costs tend to repeat weekly, monthly or perhaps annually (in the case of insurance for example). Note that entirely one-off expenses are possible, such repairing a building's roof after a severe storm, but the general rule at least helps to identify most expenses.

So whilst it is not an exact science, when looking for expenses, we are looking for outflows of cash (and sometimes other assets) from the business which occur on a regular basis and which do not generally involve the acquisition of an asset. Again, the examples given earlier satisfy these tests.

Once we have our expenses, you might recall from Abigail's business that they are recorded in ledgers just like other transactions, and that in the final accounts they appear in the profit and loss account. The profit and loss account shows the income of the business less the expenses incurred by the business to give the profit (or loss) made in the period covered by the account.

As a reminder of how an expense is recorded in the ledgers, let's assume that Brian pays the rent on his business premises. He will need to show the cash going out of his cash ledger (which, remember, will be shown as a credit entry, as the cash ledger works in the opposite way to how you might expect it to work), and a debit entry will need to be made to the rent ledger. They will look like this:

Cash

Date	Details	Dr	Cr	Balance
01/07	Rent		500	10,450dr

Rent

Date	Details	Dr	Cr	Balance
01/07	Cash	500		1,500dr

The balance in the cash ledger is just a random balance (although it shows that Brian has plenty of cash available). The rent ledger is at £1,500dr, which, if the rent is £500 per month, suggests that this is the third month that Brian has paid his rent in this accounting period. If the rent is quarterly, then this is the third quarter in which he has paid rent. (We know this because the balance of the ledger is three times the level of the rent being paid.)

Chapter 8 – Capital and Drawings

One of the first concepts we looked at in this book was the idea of capital. We saw that capital is the money (or other assets) invested into the business by its owner. Let's just revisit that and expand on it a little.

Dave wants to start a window cleaning business. He already has a van which he owns outright. He also has a ladder in the shed which he intends to use. Other bits and pieces, such as buckets and sponges, he will buy later. The van is worth £3,500, the ladder is worth £80, and he has also decided to invest another £200 in cash to get him started with the other equipment he needs.

In total, Dave is investing £3,780 into the business (the value of the van and the ladder plus the cash). All of these things will be credited to his capital ledger, to reflect his investment. The other side of each entry will depend on the nature of the thing being invested. The cash will obviously be debited (as a receipt) to the cash ledger, but the two assets (the van and the ladder) will also be debited directly to those ledgers.

The starting ledger position for Dave's business would therefore look like this, once those initial entries have been made:

Capital

Date	Details	Dr	Cr	Balance
01/08	Cash		200	200cr
01/08	Motor Vehicles		3500	3700cr
01/08	Ladders		80	3780cr

Cash

Date	Details	Dr	Cr	Balance
01/08	Capital	200		200dr

Motor Vehicles

Date	Details	Dr	Cr	Balance
01/08	Capital	3500		3500dr

Ladders

Date	Details	Dr	Cr	Balance
01/08	Capital	80		80dr

The capital ledger tells us how much the owner (Dave) has invested to start his business. The fixed asset ledgers (vehicles and ladders) tell us how much those assets cost. The cash ledger tells us how much cash the business has at its disposal.

That is the position when the business starts up and the owner invests money and other assets. Of course, at some point the owner will hope to withdraw cash from the business in order to provide a living. In other words, he or she will want to withdraw the profits from the business to reflect the effort they have put into it. Let's consider what happens in that case.

Returning to Dave, our window cleaner, let's assume that he decides to pay himself at the end of each month. We can see from the dates in the ledgers above that Dave started business on 1 August. During August he has collected cash from his customers totalling £900, which he thinks is a pretty good start. We'll assume that the balance on his cash ledger, having paid a few expenses, now stands at £1,000. Dave now decides to draw £800 from the business, believing that to be a prudent sum based on his monthly takings. Of course, he is confident that next month his takings will be higher as word gets round about his good work.

It is tempting to think that a withdrawal of money from the business in this way would be reflected by a debit entry in the capital ledger. In other words, a reversal of the entries made when the capital is first invested. However, that is not the case, and in fact a separate drawings ledger is required.

The cash being withdrawn from the business will show as a credit in the cash ledger in the usual way. For Dave, his ledgers will look like this:

Cash

Date	Details	Dr	Cr	Balance
31/08	Balance forward			1000dr
31/08	Drawings		800	200dr

Drawings

Date	Details	Dr	Cr	Balance
31/08	Cash	800		800dr

When Dave withdraws money again at the end of September, the entry will be placed into this same drawings ledger. We will see later on how the balance of this ledger is dealt with in the final accounts, but basically what happens is that the capital balance has the drawings for the year deducted from it, and the profits for the year added to it.

Capital – Drawings + Profit = Revised Capital

So we can see that Dave's investment in his business will grow if he draws less than he makes in profit, but it will shrink if he draws more than he makes in profit.

We said earlier that most businesses draw up accounts every year, so to some extent Dave will not be fully aware of his profit levels until the final accounts are constructed. In this sense there is a little 'guesswork' involved in setting his level of drawings, but he should be able to get some feel for how things are going, particularly in a relatively simple business such as his, where his expenses are quite low. His profits will consequently not be too much lower than his turnover. Remember, turnover is the amount of money that comes into Dave's business in return for providing his services. Profit, on the other hand, is what is left after he has then paid his expenses.

Profit = Income – Expenses

We have seen in this chapter how capital is the value invested into a business by its owner. Drawings are a record of what has been withdrawn, and are deducted from capital, but not until we draw up the final accounts. In the meantime, they are recorded in a drawings ledger.

Chapter 9 – The Trial Balance

We discussed the trial balance earlier in the book when we looked at Abigail's photography business. Hopefully you will recall that it is a list of the balances of all the ledgers used in the double-entry bookkeeping process within a business. In this chapter we are going to look at a more comprehensive trial balance and identify each entry and decide whether it is an item of income or expenditure, or whether it is an asset or a liability. This is a crucial step because it then helps us to see whether the item needs to appear in the profit and loss account (income and expenses), or on the balance sheet (assets and liabilities). Remember, each item in the trial balance generally appears in the final accounts once only.

We'll stick with Dave's window cleaning business for this example. Generally business has been good, and in fact Dave has recently employed Ed to help with the workload and has purchased a second van (by way of a bank loan). Assuming he has now been trading for one full year, I have set out below his trial balance. As before, note the heading, which states what it is, who it is for and the date on which it was drawn up (Dave started business on 1 August and so one year later is 31 July). Just as in the ledgers themselves, debits are shown on the left hand side and credits on the right hand side. All this statement is doing is listing the balances from the various ledgers which Dave has been creating as his business progressed (or which his accountant has produced from his business records).

Trial Balance – Dave's Window Cleaning – 31 July XXX8

Ledger	Debit (£)	Credit (£)
Cash	225	
Income		20,800
Debtors	475	
Bad Debts	200	
Sundry Expenses	200	
Wages	1,175	
Insurance	750	
Motor Vehicles	7,500	
Motor Vehicle Expenses	2,880	
Drawings	15,000	
Bank Loan		4,500
Bank Interest	425	
Ladders	250	
Capital		3,780
Totals	**29,080**	**29,080**

It balances! That's good news, and suggests that no errors have occurred. This is one role of the trial balance – it is a check on the accuracy of the ledgers. Of course, it won't identify all errors. For example, if a double entry has been missed altogether (as in, both sides of the transaction have been omitted), the trial balance will still balance. Similarly, if the wrong amount has been entered on both ledgers, then again the trial balance will still balance. The same is true if the entries are reversed – if the credit entry is entered mistakenly as a debit and vice versa, then again the trial balance will still balance, as it will if the wrong ledgers are used.

However, it will pick up other types of error, such as when one side of an entry is omitted, or if different amounts are recorded on each side of a transaction, or if a mathematical error has occurred when adding up the running balance on a ledger.

Despite this useful feature, the main purpose of the trial balance is to provide a preliminary list of ledger balances from which to create the final accounts.

Returning to Dave's trial balance, other than seeing that it balances, it is quite difficult, especially when new to accounts, to see how the business is doing. There is nothing that easily tells us how much profit he has made, and that is the purpose of the profit and loss account. It also doesn't readily tell us how his capital has been invested within the business, and that is the purpose of the balance sheet.

Having said this, it is worth looking at each entry in turn to see what it tells us and also to consider where in the final accounts it will appear.

The first entry in Dave's trial balance is taken from his cash ledger. This is probably the ledger with which we are most familiar. It is one of the most commonly used ledgers and will have an entry made to it every time the business conducts a transaction which involves the movement of cash. We've said several times already that it is an asset, a current asset to be precise, and therefore the £225 debit entry means that the business actually has £225 in cash, not that it is overdrawn (as you might expect). Remember, the increase in any asset is shown by a debit. A decrease is therefore shown by a credit. As a current asset, we know that the balance on this ledger will be shown in the balance sheet, because that is a list of the assets and liabilities of a business. It will therefore not appear in the profit and loss account (each item in the trial balance only appears once in the final accounts).

The next item on Dave's trial balance – 'Income' – is pretty easy to identify. The name is a giveaway – it is an item of income and therefore goes in the profit and loss account. Dave's income is the value of the work done for his customers, whether they have paid him yet or not. This is an important point. Dave needs to know how much work he generated for his business in this accounting period (a year). That is what the income figure will tell him. In his first year he completed work totalling £20,800. The fact that some customers have not yet paid him is not relevant to this fact. The chances are that most of them will pay him, but just haven't got round to it yet. Those people are debtors – they owe money to Dave's business. We can see the entry for debtors in the trial balance. There is £475 worth of debtors. Of course, it is important that Dave finds time to go and collect that money which he is owed at some point, otherwise it might be lost.

It is a fact of life that some of Dave's customers will never pay him. Some might move house and forget to settle up with him. Others might be unable to pay, or deliberately avoid paying him. In those cases Dave has a choice. He can write off the debt as a bad debt, or he can sue the people in question. Considering the amounts involved for each customer, he is unlikely to sue due to the relatively high legal costs that he would incur. He is therefore likely to write the amounts off as bad debts and make a note to avoid those customers in the future. Again, we can see an entry for bad debts in the trial balance – there is £200 worth of work done for which he is not going to get paid. Whilst this amount is actually still included in the total figure for income (the £20,800cr), it is then effectively reversed out by the bad debts figure (the £200dr), which is classed as an expense of the business. What this means is that Dave has a complete picture of his business. He knows what his income should have been, based on the work he completed, but he also knows the level of the bad debts. He can therefore monitor this. If the level of bad debts goes up, then he will need to think of methods of reducing them, such as requiring payment in advance for his services.

To recap so far, income is obviously income and therefore appears on the profit and loss account. We have seen that bad debts are an expense and therefore also appear on the profit and loss account. Debtors, on the other hand, are simply customers who Dave thinks will pay, but have not done so yet. They have some value; when they do pay they will provide the business with cash. Therefore they are classed as an asset – a current asset – and consequently appear on the balance sheet.

The entry labelled as sundry expenses is obviously an expense. I've included this as something which covers those bits and pieces which Dave spends but which are not really significant to be included in their own ledger. This will include soap, buckets, cloths, chamois leathers, items of stationery and so on. We've seen before that smaller assets can be classed as expenses, especially when those assets are used and replaced pretty quickly. We did this earlier in the book with the ink that Abigail was using in her photography business. Therefore, this item is an expense, and will appear in the profit and loss account.

The next item in Dave's trial balance is for wages. We know he has recently taken on Ed as an employee to help out, and so this item will be the money that Dave has paid to Ed in that respect.

Again, it is clearly an expense of the business; it is a regular payment which Dave will have to make to Ed, and is a cost to the business. Dave hopes that the work Ed will undertake will be worth more to the business than the cost of the wages he has to pay to Ed.

The next item is another expense – insurance. Again it is a regular payment and a cost to the business. Insurance is a necessity, and this item will cover insurance for the vans and perhaps public liability insurance, covering Dave (and Ed) if they happen to cause injury to someone else whilst going about their business. Again it will appear in the profit and loss account as an expense and will be a cost to the business. In other words, it will directly reduce the amount of profit that the business makes.

The next item is 'Motor Vehicles' and the amount stated is £7,500. This is not the cost of running the vans, but the cost of buying them in the first place. It is therefore not an expense, but an asset. One of the vans was introduced as part of Dave's initial capital injection. The other one was purchased with a bank loan. They are of value to the business and for use within the business and therefore satisfy our definition of an asset. They will appear as a fixed asset on the balance sheet.

Next up are the motor vehicle expenses. They will include those items which are part and parcel of running the vans, such as petrol, road tax, new tyres, repairs and MOT test costs. Insurance could also have been lumped together with these expenses, but as we have seen, Dave has recorded that cost separately. As with all other expenses, motor vehicle expenses will appear as an expense in the profit and loss account.

It is worth just thinking about motor vehicles for a moment and making sure we are clear on what is happening. We have seen that the cost of buying the vehicle in the first instance is the acquisition of an asset. Of course, Dave will still view this as a cost, or as something for which he has had to pay money, as most people do when they buy a car. However, keep in mind that what has really happened is that Dave has given up one asset (cash) in exchange for another (the vans) and so the business itself has not lost any value. Motor vehicle expenses, on the other hand, are a cost to the business, in that they result in cash leaving the business with nothing of lasting value being acquired in return. The same concepts could be applied to other assets, such as buildings. The cost of acquiring a building is the purchase of an asset. The costs of running the building are expenses.

Next on Dave's trial balance comes an entry for drawings. This is the amount of money that Dave has withdrawn from the business in order to live on. He is, after all, self-employed and needs to take money out of the business periodically to use in place of the wages he would have earned if he worked for someone else as an employee. Drawings appear on the balance sheet and are deducted from Dave's capital. We'll see how this works later.

The next item relates to the bank loan Dave has taken out to buy the second van. This appears on the credit side of the balance because the bank is a creditor for Dave's business. In other words, the bank has provided credit to Dave to allow him to buy the van from the van seller in cash. Dave owns the van (it is an asset of the business as we have seen) but he does owe the bank for the outstanding amount of the loan. The loan is therefore a liability, and it appears on the balance sheet.

The next entry is the interest which Dave has paid on the bank loan. This is the cost of borrowing the money and should therefore be recorded separately from the loan itself. As a cost, the interest is in fact an expense, and so it will appear in the profit and loss account. The loan itself does not affect the profit levels of Dave's business, as it has simply created a liability, but has also provided the business with a new asset (cash at first, and subsequently a van when Dave bought it). In theory at least, Dave could sell his van and use the proceeds to repay the loan, putting him back in the position he was in before he took the loan. Of course, this is not quite realistic as we know that the van will lose value over time (this is called depreciation and we'll look at this later). The interest, on the other hand, is a cost to the business and directly erodes Dave's profit levels.

The next item is a simple fixed asset entry for the ladders which Dave has purchased (or introduced as capital) for use in the business. Dave has decided that these are valuable enough to reflect as an asset rather than say, the buckets, which he has decided to record as an expense within the sundry expenses ledger.

The final item is the balance from Dave's capital ledger, which at this time still reflects Dave's initial investment into his business (the first van, the cash and the ladder he started with). The capital balance appears on the balance sheet where it has drawings taken away from it and profit added to it, and again we'll see how this works later when we put the balance sheet together.

So that is Dave's trial balance. As we've now seen, it is nothing overly complex, just a list of the balances from his various ledgers.

Chapter 10 – A Basic Profit and Loss Account

We looked at this earlier when we considered Abigail's photography business. Her profit and loss account was pretty straightforward, as we drew it up after she hadn't been trading for too long. Here we are going to put Dave's account together; we looked at his trial balance in the previous chapter. To a large degree, we have already undertaken the most difficult step in preparing the profit and loss account, which is to identify each figure in the trial balance as either income or expenditure, both of which appear in this account, or as an asset or liability, both of which appear on the balance sheet (we'll draw this up later).

Dave has been trading now for one year. Most businesses draw up their accounts once each year, on the same date, known as the accounting reference date.

The title for Dave's account will be 'Dave's Window Cleaning – Profit and Loss Account for the year ending 31 July XXX8'. Of course, if Dave's business has a name, then that will replace the 'Dave's Window Cleaning' part.

So now all we need to do is to set out Dave's income, and deduct his expenses. As I say, we have already identified these above, making this a relatively simple task. Once we have identified his profit, we can then put together his balance sheet.

Here goes:

Dave's Window Cleaning – Profit and Loss Account for the year ending 31 July 2018

	£	£
Income		20,800
Less: Expenses		
Motor Vehicle Expenses	2,880	
Wages	1,175	
Insurance	750	
Bank Interest	425	
Sundry Expenses	200	
Bad Debts	200	(5,630)
Net Profit		15,170

In his first year Dave has made a profit of £15,870. That is the value of the work he has done this year, less related expenses. Any purchases of assets, such as the new van, the amount of cash he has in the bank, the amount of money he owes to the bank and the amount owed to him by customers does not affect his profit – at least not directly. Of course, some of these things will have *some* effect on profit levels as we have seen. For example, the size of the loan does matter because the interest charged is an expense. The fact that some customers have not paid is also relevant, as some of those may never pay, at which point they will be a bad debt, which again will result in an expense, reducing his profit. Later in the book we will also see that assets tend to depreciate in value over time, and this also results in an expense (called depreciation).

The profit figure we are left with (often called the 'net profit' because it is net (or after) expenses, is the amount by which the business has increased in value over the course of one year. The balance sheet will reflect this increase in value, but also the fact that some (or possibly all) of this value will have been withdrawn by Dave as drawings on which to live his life outside of the business.

It is to Dave's balance sheet that we will now turn.

Chapter 11 – A Basic Balance Sheet

Again, we looked at this earlier when we considered Abigail's photography business. Remember that the balance sheet is a list of the assets and liabilities of a business, together with details of the capital invested by the owner. That is where the 'balance' part comes from, because these two things should be the same. What do I mean by this? Well, if we think about it, the money (or value) invested by the owner into the business must be the same as the current value of the assets of the business less the liabilities of the business (what it owns less what it owes to others). Or to put it another way, if all the assets in a business are sold, and the money raised is used to pay off the liabilities that are owed to others, then whatever is left should equal the amount invested by the owner. Of course this 'amount invested' by the owner will change as time goes on. We have talked already about profits being added to this amount and drawings being deducted; the balance sheet is the place where this is reflected.

The first part, or 'top half', of the balance sheet is where the assets and liabilities are shown, with fixed assets coming first, then current assets, then current liabilities and finally long term liabilities. The second part, or 'bottom half', is where the owner's capital is shown, with profits added and drawings deducted. Let's have a look at how it will be put together for Dave's business.

Balance Sheet for Dave's Window Cleaning
as at 31 July XXX8

	£	£
Employment of Capital		
Fixed Assets:		
Motor Vehicles		7,500
Ladders		250
		7,750
Current Assets:		
Debtors	475	
Cash	225	700
Net Current Assets		8,450
Long Term Liabilities:		
Bank Loan		(4,500)
Net Assets		**3,950**
Capital Employed		
Capital	3,780	
Drawings	(15,000)	
Profit	15,170	**3,950**

Good, we can see that it balances. As we saw with Abigail, the top half of the balance sheet sets out the assets and liabilities. Dave's business owns the vans and some ladders. It also has some cash and is owed £475. It doesn't have any current liabilities, but it does have a longer term liability in the bank loan. Remember, current liabilities are those liabilities that are due for payment within the next 12 months.

Note also that of the £15,170 profit which Dave's business made, he has withdrawn £15,000 to live on, leaving £170 of the profit in the business. This has been added to his capital, which has therefore increased from £3,780 to £3,950. The value of Dave's business has therefore increased by the same amount. At least in theory it has. Of course, we wouldn't really know this unless we sold off all his assets and paid off his liabilities, to see what was left. But we would expect this to be around £3,950. The other thing to keep in mind here is that when selling a business, it is often worth more than the balance sheet suggests. We might refer to the £3,950 as the "net asset value" of Dave's business, which means the value of the assets less the value of the liabilities. However, if Dave were to sell his business as a going concern (in other words, as an up and running business), he might well expect to receive more than £3,950 for it. This is because the fact that it is a profitable business makes it worth more than just the price of the assets involved. For example, Dave has probably built up a good reputation and has a list of repeat customers. This element of a business is called "goodwill" and therefore potentially has a value. However, it is usually left out of the accounts unless it has been purchased (for example, where one business buys another and the purchase price exceeds the fair value of the assets purchased to reflect the goodwill element). There are complex rules about how to account for such goodwill which are beyond the scope of a book of this nature.

Chapter 12 – Adjustments

When we talk about 'adjustments' we mean making changes to the base figures included in the trial balance. There are various circumstances that can make this necessary and we'll consider the most common adjustments in this chapter.

Firstly we'll consider the position in relation to prepayments and accruals. These can be quite tricky conceptually but are manageable with a little thought and some clear explanation. We've already talked before about the need to match payments and receipts to the period in which they relate. When we looked at Abigail's photography business right back at the beginning of the book, we discussed this when we looked at her usage of ink in her printer. We said that she was unlikely to have used all her ink during the period for which we drew up her accounts, and that the amount of ink left could be classed as a prepayment. This can occur with many different types of expense. For example, rent is often paid in advance to a landlord. If I pay a quarter's rent in advance on 1 April, then it is covering the period from 1 April until 30 June, being a three month period (one quarter). However, if I then draw up my final accounts on 31 May, not all the rent I paid relates to the period of my accounts. In fact, two months of it does (from 1 April to 31 May) and the other month does not (June). Therefore if I reflect the whole three months' worth of rent in my accounts I am overstating my expenses (and therefore understating my profit). Instead, I should include just the two months of rent that falls within the period for those accounts, and the other month of rent I have already paid is classed as a prepayment (of the rent due in the next accounting period).

Adjustments are usually given as notes to the trial balance. As they are not included in the trial balance, any adjustment of the figures that they give rise to might result in an unbalanced set of accounts. To make sure this does not happen, remember always that adjustments generally give rise to two entries in the final accounts. You will recall that we only use each item from the trial balance once in the final accounts – either in the profit and loss account or on the balance sheet, but in the case of adjustments they must appear twice to keep things balanced. More often than not, they will appear in *both* the profit and loss account and the balance sheet.

In the case of a prepayment, in our example being the rent prepaid for the month of June, the amount is deducted from the actual expense in the profit and loss account (in this case rent) so that the expense reflects the true amount that was paid and which relates to the period covered by the accounts. In addition, a current asset is created for the same amount, called simply 'prepayments', in the balance sheet. It is an asset because the business has paid out cash (for the rent in our example) and it has received something in return which is of benefit or value in the shorter term – that is, a month's future use of the building in our case (for which the rent was paid).

An accrual is similar to a prepayment but in some ways the opposite. In this case we are talking about expenses which are outstanding. For example, if it turns out that an electricity bill which has been received by a business and relates to the current accounting period has not yet been paid, then the amount due would be an accrual. In that case the actual expense for electricity in the profit and loss account would need to be increased by the amount in question, and we would need to create a current liability on the balance sheet to show that the amount is owed to someone else (the utility company).

Another type of adjustment we might make is to create a bad debt provision. We have already looked at bad debts earlier in the book, and we have seen that if a business believes that a debt owed to it will not get paid, then it should write that debt off. This has the effect of creating an expense in the profit and loss account and clearing the debt owed. This is useful for writing off specific debts owed by specific debtors. When it comes to the end of the accounting period, a business may also decide to create a general bad debt provision. By doing this, the business is recognising that a certain percentage of its debts will inevitably turn bad at some point. This is something that business owners have to live with and for which they can get a feel as they build their experience in their particular business. It is not aimed at any particular debt, but rather is there to be set off against bad debts as they arise in the future. It is a method of ensuring that the accounts produced are a true and fair reflection of how the business operates.

As with prepayments and accruals, the creation of such a bad debt provision will give rise to two effects. Firstly, it will create an expense in the profit and loss account for the amount of the provision. Secondly, the amount of the provision will be deducted from debtors on the balance sheet. Together this works to keep the final accounts balanced. The expense created means that the profit for the period will be lower, which feeds into the bottom half of the balance sheet, reducing the total there. The reduction in an asset (debtors) on the balance sheet means that the top half of the balance sheet will also be lower by the same amount, maintaining the balance.

Another common adjustment is that made for depreciation. Depreciation is an amount which is deducted from the book value of certain fixed assets in order to reflect the fact that those assets are reducing in value. For example, if we think about Dave's van which he purchased for use in his window cleaning business, we know that the van will gradually lose value over time as he uses it (and even if he didn't use it). In order to give a true and fair view of the value of the business, the accounts must reflect this depreciation.

Businesses value depreciation in different ways, and there is an element of choice to some extent, but it must be realistic. Often it is done on a percentage basis, so that each year say 20 per cent of the value of the asset is taken as the figure for depreciation. This percentage can be applied either to the original purchase price (called the straight line basis, because it gives the same amount of depreciation each year), or to the current value of the asset as reflected in the accounts after any previous depreciation has been deducted (called the reducing balance basis, as the amount of depreciation tends to fall as time goes on). We'll see an example of how this works later in the book.

Again this gives rise to two entries. Firstly, the depreciation for the current year is deducted as an expense in the profit and loss account to which it relates. Secondly, it is also deducted from the value of the asset on the balance sheet. Again, these two entries work together to keep the accounts balanced. Note that the balance sheet depreciation will build up over time, so that the full amount of depreciation from all previous years (and the current year) will be deducted here, although the profit and loss account will only show the expense of this current year's depreciation. Once the value of the asset has reached zero, no further depreciation need be accounted for.

Depreciation is quite a difficult concept to understand. In its basic form it is relatively simple and it is fairly easy to see the rationale for it. However, note that nothing we have said so far has resulted in any cash being stored in order to replace the asset in question. Depreciation is not about building up a reserve of cash to use to purchase a replacement asset. This must be done separately by the business (for example, by opening a separate bank account and moving cash into it). All depreciation is doing is making sure that the value of the business is not overstated in the accounts, which must show a true and fair view of the financial health of the business. As depreciation is deducted from the asset's original value in the balance sheet, it helps to do just that, by reducing the asset's stated value (or *book value*) over time.

The final adjustment is the one made for closing stock. Again we have touched on this before when we looked at Alice's gift shop business earlier in the book. We noted that her purchases of stock (things she sold in her shop) would be recorded in a purchases ledger, and that sales of her stock would be recorded in a sales ledger. We noticed that there is therefore no record of current stock levels, only of the values of stock purchased and stock sold. Since stock would most likely be sold at a different (higher) price than which it was purchased for, we could never be sure from looking at those records how much physical stock Alice had at any one time. That is where we looked at the stocktake.

By conducting a stocktake, a business owner is counting up and valuing the stock in their business as the end of the accounting period, in readiness for the end of year accounts. Once this value has been established, it will be entered onto the balance sheet as a current asset (being an asset which will hopefully sell within the next 12 months). The other entry for this adjustment is made at the top of the profit and loss account where it adjusts the income made by the business. We'll look at exactly how this works in the next chapter.

Chapter 13 – A Final Example

In this chapter we are going to go through one last full example. The business in question is a trading business, so the example will include accounting entries for purchases as well as opening and closing stock. That will give us a chance to look in more detail at the top of the profit and loss account or, to put it another way, at the trading account.

A trading account is where we work out the gross profit of a business. In this account the purchases (of stock) made by a business in an accounting period are deducted from the sales (of stock) made by that business in the same period. However, to give a true picture of what the gross profit should be, we must also take into account the stock which was in the business at the start of the year (the opening stock) and also the stock in the business at the end of the year (the closing stock).

The business in question is called ABC Furniture. It buys furniture from a wholesaler and sells it through a retail outlet that is rented from a landlord. The owner of ABC Furniture is called Emma. Emma has been trading for some years now, so this is not her first set of accounts. We'll consider the impact of this as we go along. But first of all, let's have a look at the trial balance for ABC Furniture.

Trial Balance for ABC Furniture as at 31 October XXX8

Ledger	Debit (£)	Credit (£)
Cash		4,300
Sales		170,600
Purchases	42,000	
Opening Stock	35,000	
Debtors	26,200	
Creditors		27,500
Bad Debts	2,700	
Sundry Expenses	2,500	
Wages	52,000	
Insurance	2,800	
Motor Vehicles	15,000	
Motor Vehicle Depreciation		5,400
Motor Vehicle Expenses	3,200	
Rent	15,000	
Power	4,000	
Drawings	29,800	
Bank Loan		3,500
Bank Interest	300	
Shop Fittings	6,000	
Shop Fitting Depreciation		1,200
Capital		24,000
Totals	**236,500**	**236,500**

As we would expect, it balances. Hopefully
you are in a position already to look down the list
and begin to recognise these entries as assets,
liabilities, income and expenses, but we'll look at this

in more detail soon. We are also given the following information about Emma's business:

1. She has completed a stocktake and she has valued her closing stock at the end of the period at £37,000.

2. Based on previous experience, she has made a further provision for bad debts of £2,000.

3. She has found an unpaid utility bill which relates to the period of these accounts. The bill is for £500.

4. £800 of the insurance expense relates to the next accounting period because the policy runs into the next period but Emma has already paid in full.

5. Each year, Emma depreciates her motor vehicles by 20 per cent on a reducing balance basis, and her shop fittings by 10 per cent of their original cost.

So now we have all the information we need, we can begin to put the final accounts together for Emma's business. Many of the entries should be familiar to you by now. If we scan for income items, we can see that there is no 'income' ledger balance as such, but there is an entry for sales. This will reflect the value of sales of furniture made in the accounting period, which as we know will usually be a year. The sales figure in a trading business such as this, which buys and sells stock, replaces the income figure which is often found in businesses that provide a service, like Abigail's photography business and Dave's window cleaning business.

Looking now for expenses, we can see the usual kind of recurring expenditure which many businesses face. From the top, we can pull out sundry expenses, wages, insurance, motor vehicle expenses, rent, power (electricity and gas) and bank interest as being more obvious expenses. However, we also know that bad debts appear as an expense too. In addition, we now know that from the adjustment information at the bottom of the trial balance, there will be an expense for the bad debt provision and for the depreciation from this current year.

If we are looking for fixed assets, then we can see that the business owns motor vehicles and shop fittings. Remember, these are assets which the business has purchased to use within the business, not with a view to sell them quickly for a profit. We know that the depreciation figures will impact on the value of these assets.

Current assets are those which are expected to turn into cash in the next 12 months. The most obvious here are the debtors (generally people who owe money to the business for goods they have purchased on credit and are yet to pay for). We know that this figure will be reduced by the creation of the bad debt provision. We also now know that the prepayment of the insurance will give rise to a current asset too, as will the closing stock figure that Emma has come to when valuing her stock at the end of the year. We would normally expect to see cash as a current asset, but in this case, notice that the cash ledger balance is a credit balance. Can you recall that a credit balance actually means that the balance is in fact 'overdrawn'? If this ledger truly reflects the bank account for the business, then the bank account will be overdrawn too. That is not necessarily a bad thing, and Emma will no doubt have agreed this with her bank, but it does mean that she is probably paying interest on that overdrawn balance. So in this case, the cash balance is in fact a current liability as a debt which is due to the bank within the next 12 months (at least in theory – in practice the bank may well be happy for the overdraft to go beyond this timeframe).

As well as the bank overdraft, the entry for creditors is also a current liability. You will recall that creditors often relate to purchases of stock which the business has made on credit and for which it is yet to pay. In addition, we know that the accrual of the utility bill will also create a liability (the bill is due to be paid soon).

As before, we'll treat the bank loan as a long term liability, due in more than 12 months' time.

So that deals with most of the entries, so what do we have left? Well, there is the capital and the drawings, but as we've seen before they are dealt with at the end of the balance sheet, reflecting the amount that Emma has invested into the business (capital) and the amount she has withdrawn from the business to live on for this period (drawings). We'll also be adding the net profit into this part of the balance sheet once we have worked it out in the profit and loss account.

That then just leaves purchases and opening stock. These two items are used at the start of the profit and loss account, in the trading account, to work out the true income position of Emma's business. We haven't seen how that works yet, so we'll turn to that now, which is a good place to start putting the accounts together. It is worth noting here that the trading account often tends not to have a separate heading.

Starting as ever at the top of the profit and loss account, we first need to look for items of income. We've already highlighted the sales figure as being the value of stock sold by the business in this accounting year. So we can start our profit and loss account as follows:

Profit and Loss Account of ABC Furniture for the year ending 31 October XXX8

	£
Sales	170,600

What we need to do now is make this into a trading account, in which we work out Emma's gross profit. Gross profit for a business is the value of the sales less the amount which was paid for those sales. It is the basic profit made on the sale of stock in a business before other expenses are deducted. It is a useful figure to know, as it can be compared with previous years' figures to help assess pricing strategies. Whilst some other expenses might be beyond the control of the business, the level of its pricing is something it can at least have some control over.

We know the amount which Emma spent on stock this year, as that is the purchases figure of £42,000. It might be tempting to think therefore that her gross profit is £170,600 less £42,000, which would give us £128,600. However, it is not as simple as that. This is because Emma had some stock at the start of the year and some stock at the end of the year. The cost of the stock she sold therefore does not necessarily (and in fact is very unlikely to) match exactly the cost of the stock she bought. This would only be the case if her opening stock was valued at exactly the same as her closing stock which, as we can see from the trial balance and the adjustment information below it, it isn't.

What has actually happened is that her level of stock has gone up by £2,000. The opening stock at the start of the period was £35,000 and the closing stock at the end of the period is £37,000. We therefore need to adjust the purchases figure accordingly. Let's see how that works.

Profit and Loss Account of ABC Furniture for the year ending 31 October XXX8

	£	£
Sales		170,600
Less: Cost of Goods Sold		
Opening Stock	35,000	
Add Purchases	42,000	
	77,000	
Less Closing Stock	(37,000)	(40,000)
Gross Profit		**130,600**

You can see that we have added in a new stage here, in which we are calculating the cost of goods sold. That is an important step in calculating the gross profit for a trading business. We need to know the value of the stock sold in the period, which is the sales figure. From that we need to take the amount that was paid for the stock that has been sold. So this is not just the purchases figure. What this trading account does, when calculating the cost of the goods sold in the period, is to start with the value of the opening stock, add the purchases, and then deduct the closing stock. I remember this by thinking that what we are doing is assuming that the opening stock has been sold, along with the purchases made during the year, but that we are left with the closing stock. Of course, the actual closing stock is likely to include items which have been purchased during the year, and even items which were in stock at the start of the year, but for the accounts that doesn't really matter. What is important is the *value* of these things. As a reminder, the closing stock will be valued at the *lower* of its acquisition cost or its realisable value. We saw this in action earlier in the book when we looked at Alice's gift shop business. What this does mean is that if there is stock left in the business from last year, the owner must decide what value to place on this 'old' stock, and may well need to value it lower than its actual cost, on the basis that it is unlikely to *realise* that amount when it is sold (if it can even be sold).

The next thing we need to do for ABC Furniture is to list its expenses and deduct those from the gross profit to give the net profit (as in, the profit net of, or *after*, expenses). We have already identified those expenses as being the sundry expenses, wages, insurance, motor vehicle expenses, rent, power (electricity and gas), bank interest, bad debts, bad debt provision and also the depreciation from this current year. Remember, Emma has chosen to depreciate her vehicles at 20 per cent on a reducing balance basis. That means we need to work out the current *book value* of the vehicles and then apply the rate of depreciation. The trial balance tells us that Emma has spent £15,000 on vehicles, and also that she has already depreciated them by £5,400. That means the current value as stated in the accounts is £15,000 less £5,400, which gives £9,600. We then depreciate this *reduced balance* by the 20 per cent rate of depreciation to give depreciation of £1,920. This amount is the expense for motor vehicle depreciation that we need in this year's profit and loss account. It will also be added to the existing accumulated depreciation (of £5,400) which is then deducted from the value of the asset in the balance sheet to show a revised current *book value*.

The shop fittings are also depreciated, this time by 10 per cent of their original cost. Their cost is shown as £6,000 in the trial balance, and so £600 will be depreciated each year. Again, this will be an expense in the profit and loss account and also added to the existing accumulated depreciation (of £1,200) which in turn is deducted from the value of the shop fittings in the balance sheet to give a revised current book value for the asset.

Let's put the expenses into her profit and loss account.

Profit and Loss Account of ABC Furniture for the year ending 31 October XXX8

	£	£	£
Sales			170,600
Less: Cost of Goods Sold			
Opening Stock		35,000	
Add Purchases		42,000	
		77,000	
Less Closing Stock		(37,000)	(40,000)
Gross Profit			**130,600**
Less: Expenses			
Wages		52,000	
Rent		15,000	
Power	4,000		
Add accrual	500	4,500	
Motor Expenses		3,200	
Insurance	2,800		
Less prepayment	(800)	2,000	
Sundry Expenses		2,500	
Bank Interest		300	
Bad Debts		2,700	
Bad Debt Provision		2,000	
Shop fittings depreciation		600	
Vehicle depreciation		1,920	(86,720)
Net Profit			**43,880**

You will notice that we have moved to three columns in this version of the profit and loss account. That is mainly due to the accrual and the prepayment. The accrual is the utility bill that Emma found that has not yet been paid, even though it relates to the period for these accounts. It therefore needs to be added on to the relevant expense (power). To do this clearly, we need to move inside one column to do the adjustment, before taking the revised total for the power expense (£4,500) back into the main expenses column in the centre. The same applies to the insurance expense, although in that case the prepayment has been deducted, as it relates to the next accounting period, not this one. Both the accrual and the expense will also appear on the balance sheet, as we shall see in due course.

We can also see that Emma's net profit for this period is £43,880. It seems like a good amount of profit, but there are a number of factors which can help us to determine whether that is actually the case.

Firstly, we could compare it to Emma's previous results. If she made £53,000 profit last year, then we might view this year's profits as disappointing. On the other hand, if she made £33,000 last year, then we might be pleased with this year's result.

Secondly, we could compare the profit levels to other businesses of the same type and size. If other small furniture businesses are making six-figure profit levels then Emma might validly consider why she isn't doing the same. Of course, it might be difficult to find out what other businesses are doing, but professional advisers or trade contacts might be able to shed some light on this.

Finally, we could ask Emma herself whether she is happy with her levels of profit. Of course, many other factors come into play here; she might be actively trying to expand, in which case she would be disappointed by anything other than a significant increase in profits. Or she might be winding down for retirement, or in a recession, in which case she might be untroubled by a drop in profits. She will also be aware of any other business factors which might have had an impact this year's performance.

Now that we have completed the profit and loss account, we can turn to the balance sheet for Emma's business. You will recall that we must first list the fixed assets of ABC Furniture. These are assets which are used within the business, usually on a long term basis, to help generate profits. They are not assets which were purchased with a view to selling them for a profit. For ABC Furniture, we can identify the motor vehicles and the shop fittings.

We are also told, in the information set out after her trial balance, that Emma depreciates her motor vehicles and her shop fittings. We have seen that the original cost of Emma's vehicles is stated to be £15,000. There is then an entry for accumulated depreciation (£5,400). This is the depreciation that Emma has already accounted for in *previous* years' accounts. Therefore, the position at the *start* of the period that we are now looking at is that she had spent £15,000 on motor vehicles, and had depreciated them by £5,400. We could say then, that the *book value* of the motor vehicles at that time was £9,600. Similarly, the value of the shop fittings at the start of the period was the original cost of £6,000 stated in the trial balance, less the £1,200 of accumulated depreciation, leaving a starting book value of £4,800.

For the current year, we have seen above that both assets have been further depreciated by £1,920 and £600 respectively. These amounts need to be added to the existing accumulated depreciation and then deducted from the cost of the assets to give their current, *end* of period book values. This is how that will look at the start of the balance sheet:

Balance Sheet for ABC Furniture as at 31 October XXX8

	£	£	£
Employment of Capital			
Fixed Assets:			
Motor Vehicles		15,000	
Less accumulated depreciation		(7,320)	7,680
Shop fittings		6,000	
Less accumulated depreciation		1,800	4,200
			11,880

That deals with the fixed assets of the business. You can see that the vehicles are shown at their cost value of £15,000 (that is, what Emma paid for them originally) less their accumulated depreciation to date. That figure of £7,320 is made up of the accumulated depreciation from previous years (£5,400) *and* the depreciation for this current year that we calculated earlier for the profit and loss account (£1,920). The current book values of the vehicles and the fittings are therefore £7,680 and £4,200 respectively. Remember, these are unlikely to reflect the *actual* values of those assets, but they should at least give a fair view of the values, having been subjected to reasonable rates of depreciation.

Next up we need to add in the current assets of the business. We have already identified these earlier on as being the debtors (people who owe money to the business) and the prepayment of the insurance. We can add to this list the closing stock figure from the information given to us after the trial balance. Remember, this figure has been established by Emma as a result of her stocktake at the end of the accounting period.

Adding in the current assets will look like this:

Balance Sheet for ABC Furniture as at 31 October XXX8

	£	£	£
Employment of Capital			
Fixed Assets:			
Motor Vehicles		15,000	
Less accumulated depreciation		(7,320)	7,680
Shop fittings		6,000	
Less accumulated depreciation		1,800	4,200
			11,880
Current Assets:			
Closing stock		37,000	
Debtors	26,200		
Less bad debt provision	(2,000)	24,200	
Prepayment of insurance		800	
		62,000	

So here we have just listed the current assets and added them up at the bottom of the list. We've had to use a third column again here, as we did on the profit and loss account, in order to show the adjustment of the debtors to take into account the newly created bad debt provision. We found this information in the notes at the bottom of the trial balance. This is the amount of her existing debtors that Emma believes, based on experience, will become bad in due course. She hasn't necessarily identified any particular debtor who won't pay (if she had, then she could have written this off already, thereby increasing her bad debts). Here she is just being prudent, and showing that she expects not to receive all the money that is due to her. Again, it is about making sure the accounts show a true and fair view of her business.

Next, we need to take off the liabilities of the business. We'll introduce the current liabilities that we identified earlier (the overdraft, the creditors and the accrual of the unpaid utility bill) and the long term liability of the bank loan here. In fact, we'll finish of the balance sheet by including the bottom half of the statement which shows Emma's investment in the business. I'll explain it after we've done that.

It will look like this:

Balance Sheet for ABC Furniture as at 31 October XXX8

	£	£	£
Employment of Capital			
Fixed Assets:			
Motor Vehicles		15,000	
Less accumulated depreciation		(7,320)	7,680
Shop fittings		6,000	
Less accumulated depreciation		1,800	4,200
			11,880
Current Assets:			
Closing stock		37,000	
Debtors	26,200		
Less bad debt provision	(2,000)	24,200	
Prepayment of insurance		800	
		62,000	
Less current liabilities:			
Creditors		27,500	
Accrual of utility bill		500	
Bank overdraft		4,300	
		(32,300)	
Net Current Assets			29,700
Long Term Liabilities:			
Bank Loan			(3,500)
Net Assets			**38,080**
Capital Employed			
Capital	24,000		
Drawings	(29,800)		
Profit	43,880		**38,080**

We can see that the balance sheet balances, in that the total of all the assets less the liabilities gives the figure of £38,080 (the 'Net Assets'). In addition, the total of Emma's investment is now £38,080. This is made up of her starting capital of £24,000, from which we have deducted her drawings of £29,800 and added her profit for the year from the profit and loss account of £43,880.

In theory, if we sold all the assets of the business and paid off all the debts, we would be left with £38,080, which we would then give to Emma to return her investment. Of course, this might not work out exactly as planned, as the assets might not sell for the values in the balance sheet, but it certainly gives us a 'true and fair' view of Emma's business.

Chapter 14 – Service Providers

This chapter is a short chapter in which we will return to something we discussed earlier in the book. In the example we considered for ABC Furniture, we were dealing with a trading business. In other words, Emma bought and sold stock (furniture) to make a profit. We've talked before about businesses which provide a service rather than buy and sell stock. We could think back here to Abigail and her photography business. The reason we are returning to that now is just to clarify one thing. We said that service providers like Abigail do not have stock, and therefore do not have opening and closing stock, or sales and purchases in the same way that a trading business does. We saw that service providers have income and work in progress instead. Here I just want to clarify how those entries will impact on the final accounts.

The trial balance will include a figure for the opening work in progress. The business owner would then need to value the closing work in progress outstanding at the end of the period. We talked about this earlier in Chapter 5. If, in her second year of business, Abigail had income of £35,000, opening work in progress of £1,500, and closing work in progress of £1,000, then the start of her profit and loss account would look like this:

Profit and Loss Account for Abigail Photography for the period ending 31 May XXX3

	£	£
Income	35,000	
Less Opening Work in Progress	(1,500)	
Add Closing Work in Progress	1,000	34,500

Less: Expenses…

You can see that it is not *too* different to the trading account (the start of the profit and loss account for a trading business). The basis for the adjustment is that the income figure should only include income that relates to the period for which the accounts are being drawn up. Any work in progress in existence at the start of the period will of course actually relate to work carried out in the *previous* period. Therefore it should be deducted, because it will have been billed for and included in the income total but it doesn't belong in this period. Any work in progress in existence at the end of the period will naturally relate to the current period, and therefore needs to be added on – it will not have been billed for yet, but it does belong in this period. One period's closing work in progress will be the next period's opening work in progress.

Other than that, the profit and loss account will be the same as it was for a trading business.

When it comes to the balance sheet, the closing work in progress will appear as a current asset, in the same way as the closing stock for a trading business would have done. Again, other than that, the balance sheet will be the same.

Chapter 15 – Value Added Tax

This chapter will briefly cover the accounting treatment of value added tax or, as it is usually known, VAT. It is not the aim of this book to cover this tax in detail, but it would not be complete without some mention of it.

VAT is a tax which must be accounted for by any business which is VAT registered. Such a business must effectively charge the tax to its own customers and then account for it to HM Revenue and Customs, usually on a quarterly basis.

Let's assume that Emma (our furniture seller) is registered for VAT. If she sells a piece of furniture for £1,000, then she will have to charge VAT at the current rate (20 per cent at the time of writing). That means she will actually charge her customer £1,200 for the furniture. However, note that Emma cannot record the whole total as her sale. She can credit her sales ledger with £1,000, as that is the true value of the furniture sold. She then needs to show the receipt of that cash in her cash ledger, so that can be debited by £1,000 (remember that the cash ledger is debited to show money being received). The £200 in respect of VAT is still cash that she has received from her customer, and so needs to be debited to the cash ledger, but in that case the 'other side' of the entry is credited to her VAT ledger.

This is how that will look:

Cash

Date	Details	Dr	Cr	Balance
12/07	Sales	1,000		1,000dr
12/07	VAT	200		1,200dr

Sales

Date	Details	Dr	Cr	Balance
12/07	Cash		1,000	1,000cr

VAT

Date	Details	Dr	Cr	Balance
12/07	Cash		200	200cr

VAT registered businesses can often also set off the VAT they incur on purchases against the VAT they must account for on their sales. In that case a similar set of entries will be made when purchases are made, but they will be the opposite of the ones above.

For example, if Emma purchases a piece of furniture for £500 plus VAT, then she will pay £600 in total to her supplier. £500 of this is the true value of the furniture without the VAT, and £100 relates to the VAT (20 per cent of £500). Emma will credit her cash

ledger with £500 and debit her purchases ledger in
the usual way, and then she will also credit her cash
ledger with £100 and debit her VAT ledger with £100.
The entries will look like this:

Cash

Date	Details	Dr	Cr	Balance
12/07	Sales	1,000		1,000dr
12/07	VAT	200		1,200dr
13/07	Purchases		500	700dr
13/07	VAT		100	600dr

Sales

Date	Details	Dr	Cr	Balance
12/07	Cash		1,000	1,000cr

Purchases

Date	Details	Dr	Cr	Balance
13/07	Cash	500		500dr

VAT

Date	Details	Dr	Cr	Balance
12/07	Cash		200	200cr
13/07	Cash	100		100dr

We can see from this that Emma now owes
£100 of VAT (the balance on her VAT ledger). She has
made sales of £1,000 and purchases of £500. She also

has £600 in her cash account, £500 of which is hers to keep being the difference between her sales and purchases, and £100 of which should be kept aside in order to pay her VAT account to HM Revenue and Customs when it falls due (this is made up of the £200 she collected on her sale less the £100 she paid on her purchase and which she is allowed to set off).

When it comes to drawing up her final accounts, the balances on her cash, sales and purchases ledgers will be dealt with in exactly the same way as we have seen earlier in the book. The balance on her VAT ledger will be shown as a current liability on the balance sheet as it will generally be due to HM Revenue and Customs within the next 12 months (because VAT is usually paid quarterly).

When the time comes to pay the VAT to HM Revenue and Customs, then Emma simply credits the cash account to show the cash going out of the business, and debits the VAT account to clear the balance due.

Chapter 16 – Interpreting Accounts

So far this book has looked at how to record accounting information and how to use that information to prepare the final accounts of a small business. This chapter aims to introduce you briefly to the concept of interpreting accounts. In other words, what do the accounts actually tell us?

The main method used to assist in this process is ratio analysis. A ratio is simply a comparison between two numbers. If a bag of sweets contains 30 red sweets and 10 blue sweets, then we could say the ratio of red to blue sweets is 30:10. This is pronounced "thirty to ten". That means that for every 30 red sweets there are 10 blue sweets. We could simplify this further by dividing each side by 10, so that the ratio becomes 3:1 ("three to one"). In other words, for every three red sweets in the bag, there is one blue sweet.

Ratio analysis of accounts is therefore about comparing different numbers with each other. There are dozens, if not hundreds, of potential ratios we could calculate, all of which would probably tell us *something* useful. However, there are certain common ratios which are very useful and this chapter will focus on some of these more common ratios.

For ease of reference, here are the accounts for ABC Furniture that we prepared earlier:

Profit and Loss Account of ABC Furniture for the year ending 31 October XXX8

	£	£	£
Sales			170,600
Less: Cost of Goods Sold			
Opening Stock		35,000	
Add Purchases		42,000	
		77,000	
Less Closing Stock		(37,000)	(40,000)
Gross Profit			**130,600**
Less: Expenses			
Wages		52,000	
Rent		15,000	
Power	4,000		
Add accrual	500	4,500	
Motor Expenses		3,200	
Insurance	2,800		
Less prepayment	(800)	2,000	
Sundry Expenses		2,500	
Bank Interest		300	
Bad Debts		2,700	
Bad Debt Provision		2,000	
Shop fittings depreciation		600	
Vehicle depreciation		1,920	(86,720)
Net Profit			**43,880**

Balance Sheet for ABC Furniture as at 31 October XXX8

	£	£	£
Employment of Capital			
Fixed Assets:			
Motor Vehicles		15,000	
Less accumulated depreciation		(7,320)	7,680
Shop fittings		6,000	
Less accumulated depreciation		1,800	4,200
			11,880
Current Assets:			
Closing stock		37,000	
Debtors	26,200		
Less bad debt provision	(2,000)	24,200	
Prepayment of insurance		800	
		62,000	
Less current liabilities:			
Creditors		27,500	
Accrual of utility bill		500	
Bank overdraft		4,300	
		(32,300)	
Net Current Assets			29,700
Long Term Liabilities:			
Bank Loan			(3,500)
Net Assets			**38,080**
Capital Employed			
Capital	24,000		
Drawings	(29,800)		
Profit	43,880		**38,080**

The first ratio I want to consider is called the current asset ratio. This compares the current assets of a business to its current liabilities. If we do this for the accounts of ABC Furniture, we get the following ratio, by taking the figures for current assets and current liabilities from the balance sheet:

62,000 : 32,300

Ratios are easier to understand if we express them as "something to one" or X : 1. To do this, simply divide the first number by the second and write ": 1" after the result. 62,000 divided by 32,300 gives 1.92 (rounded to two decimal places for clarity). We can therefore say that the current asset ratio for ABC Furniture is 1.92:1.

What does this tell us? Well, you probably recall that current assets are assets which are either cash, or are likely to generate cash by the business in the next 12 months. Similarly, current liabilities are liabilities which generally need to be paid by the business within the next 12 months. The current asset ratio compares the two together. In this case it tells us that for every £1 of current liabilities, the business has £1.92 worth of current assets. So in this case, Emma can be fairly happy that as her current liabilities become due for payment, she will have enough cash to meet them. In that sense, we would usually hope to see a current asset ratio of more than 1:1, but preferably one that is more like 1.5:1 or even better (as in this case). A low ratio may suggest that the business will struggle to pay its liabilities as they fall due, which in itself can be evidence of insolvency. Acceptable levels of this ratio will of course vary from business to business and from industry to industry.

Another useful ratio is the acid test ratio. This ratio is exactly the same as the current asset ratio, but it takes stock out of the calculation. For ABC Furniture then, the current assets without including the stock add up to £25,000. Comparing this to the current liabilities gives a ratio of:

25,000 : 32,300 or 0.77 :1

This ratio will be lower than the current asset ratio, but we would usually like to see this at 1:1. Why do we take stock out of this ratio? The answer is that stock is the most difficult current asset to turn into cash. It needs to be sold and paid for, and that might not always be easy. The ratio for ABC Furniture is a little on the low side, but as long as it keeps selling its stock, then it should be able to pay its current liabilities as they fall due.

Another ratio which can be useful is called the return on capital employed. The purpose of this ratio is to inform the business owner about the rate of return they are obtaining, based on the level of investment they have made into the business and the level of profit being made. It compares the total capital employed to the net profit figure. In the case of ABC Furniture, we can see that Emma has invested a total of £38,080 (from the bottom of the balance sheet). Her net profit for the year was £43,880. Therefore her return on capital employed is 43,880 divided by 38,080, which gives 1.15. Note that in this case we are talking about a rate of return, so rather than expressing this figure as a ratio, we express it as a percentage. Emma's return is therefore 115% (multiply the result by 100). In other words, her profit is 115% of her total investment. That seems like a good rate of return, but this is a ratio that really needs to be compared to previous years' ratios in order to comment validly. If she is maintaining the level of previous years' ratios or even improving on them, then that is good. This rate of return also allows Emma to compare this investment with other forms of investment. For example, by looking at the different returns on capital employed from different types of business she can assess whether her business is a good investment (something she hopefully tried to forecast before she actually started out!).

Another useful ratio is to compare the debtors of a business with its sales. This helps to determine how efficiently the business is collecting its debts. For ABC Furniture, the debtors are £24,200 (in the balance sheet) and the sales are £170,600 (in the profit and loss account). Again, this is not actually expressed as a ratio. Instead, the result is multiplied by 365 to give a number of days. For ABC Furniture that works out as follows:

24,200 divided by 170,600 x 365 = 52 days

So it is taking Emma 52 days to collect the debts due to her business. This might seem a little high (most trade credit tends to be around 30 days after all), but if we consider the nature of what she sells, then it might well be perfectly acceptable. Furniture is something which people often buy on longer agreed credit terms. It is likely that Emma allows people to pay her over the course of several months or even longer. If that is the case, then the longer 'average collection period' as it is known, is nothing to worry about. On the other hand, if her agreed credit terms are just 30 days, then she needs to tighten her credit control processes and try to make her debtors pay for their furniture more quickly.

The final ratio that I want to look at here is called the 'average payment period' and goes hand in hand with the ratio discussed above. This time we are checking how long it is taking a business to pay its own debts, rather than collect in debts from others. That requires us to compare the creditors of the business to its purchases and again multiply the result by 365. For ABC Furniture, that gives:

27,500 divided by 47,000 x 365 = 214 days

This seems like rather a long time, but again the nature of Emma's business (furniture) may well have an impact here. It is likely that she is getting generous credit terms on her own purchases of stock from her suppliers. If not, then this is something that needs to be addressed quickly, as one of those suppliers might lose their patience and start costly court proceedings against the business. In addition, Emma might be suffering high interest charges on those outstanding creditors, but we would need further information to be sure.

As I alluded to at the start of this chapter, there are many different ratios which provide wide and detailed information about a business. We have looked at five of the most common ratios in this chapter, and that is probably sufficient for an introductory book of this nature.

CPSIA information can be obtained
at www.ICGtesting.com
Printed in the USA
LVHW081632080121
676074LV00039B/1288